THE IDEAL MAN 101

THE IDEAL MAN 101

MARY ELLA THROENER

LIBRARY OF CONGRESS CONTROL NUMBER:		2020921989
ISBN:	HARDCOVER	978-1-6641-4117-9
	SOFTCOVER	978-1-6641-4116-2
	EBOOK	978-1-6641-4118-6

Scripture quotations marked NASB are taken from the New American Standard Bible®, Copyright © 1960, 1962, 1963, 1968, 1971, 1972, 1973, 1975, 1977, 1995 by The Lockman Foundation. Used by permission.

Any people depicted in stock imagery provided by Getty Images are models, and such images are being used for illustrative purposes only.
Certain stock imagery © Getty Images.

Print information available on the last page.

Rev. date: 11/09/2020

To order additional copies of this book, contact:
Xlibris
844-714-8691
www.Xlibris.com
Orders@Xlibris.com
816271

CONTENTS

Introduction vii

Dream of the Ideal Man.. 1
Why 101? 2
Days to Pentecost... 4
Days in the Desert 5
Days to Easter... 6
Books of the New Testament Bible 7

      The Gospels 7
      New Testament Letters 11
      Catholic Letters.. 16

The Stations of the Cross... 20
Works of Mercy 24
The Last Supper.. 29
The Apostles.. 30
The Fruits of the Holy Spirit.. 34
The Ten Commandments are Laws of Love... 39
The Ten Commandments... 45
The New Testament Writers 46
The Beatitudes... 49
The Capital Sins.. 52
The Deacons 54
The Gifts of the Holy Spirit.. 56
The Last Words of Christ 60
The Moral Virtues 62
The Sacraments 65
The Unities of the Church 69
The Rosary... 72

      The Glorious Mysteries of the Rosary... 72
      The Joyful Mysteries of the Rosary 73
      The Luminous Mysteries of the Rosary... 74
      The Sorrowful Mysteries of the Rosary... 75

The Cardinal Virtues 77
The Ends (Winds) of the Earth 79
The Marks of the Church 80
Essential Relationships 81
The Theological Virtues 82
God 84
Why 101? 87

Introduction

How can we truly be and become who God wants us to be? The purpose of this book is to hopefully help others come to love His word, the Bible, in a renewed or in a new way more than ever before! It is written from the perspective of what value and good *numbers* can be in a person's day-in and day-out living. It also has an open means of continuing to learn and grow by researching and taking ownership of the meaning and value of numbers with regard to several aspects of life. The book is for Christian adults who want to learn and do better in this world. It could also be used as youth study the Bible in their high school years.

In my childhood, I wasn't too familiar with the book, the Bible. I remember when I was around seven years old, I sneaked into my parents' room and tried to read my mom's Protestant Bible. Well, that got me in trouble, so I just remained curious on why that was not a good thing to do. As I began to research that for myself in high school years, I began to yearn to know about this great book! This continues today and at times more than other times over the years. Being at church for the Bible readings or God's many messages for me is such a *gift*! Since I believe I have received such a gift, I feel that I should share with others some of what I have been given! Please pray for me so it continues each day that I search and strive to be and become who God wants me to be.

Dream of the Ideal Man

Would you like to be known as the *ideal man* in this world?
Would you like to be known as the *ideal man* of your family?
Would you like to be known as the *ideal man* of your church?
Would you like to be known as the *ideal man* of your workplace?

Who is the *ideal man* of this world, of the family, of the church, and of the workplace? *Jesus Christ* is the ideal man.

How well do we know Him?
How well do we love Him?
How well do we serve Him?

Who was chosen to have the gift and wisdom to participate
in this life and begin this life of this ideal man? Jesus.

Because of Jesus, we hope to live this life on our way to the next life in heaven!

An *ideal woman*, Mary, His mother, was chosen.

Why 101?

God is our number one in the beginning.
God is our center in the middle.
God is our number one in the end.

101

Numbers keep order in our life
Numbers help us have discipline in our life.
Numbers help us have dreams and a vision.

So when did we first learn our numbers? How well do we know our numbers as adults in our faith life and especially from the Bible, the inspired word of God? Are we in preschool, elementary, high school, college, or beyond? How well does the ideal man know his numbers and share them with others in the best book, the Bible?

In the Old Testament, in the book titled Numbers, we have a census taking place, in which the number of people were being counted. These people were known as the Israelites. What was the purpose for these numbers? This fourth book in the Old Testament speaks a lot about laws and history. How much do we know? I missed the study of salvation history in my youth. I just wasn't in a class where it was taught, and I didn't do any independent study on it. I had an attitude that history was boring, so why waste my time on it? ("Father, forgive me, because I still do not know much salvation history.")

As we begin focusing on numbers, let us see what ways we are making God number one *in our communications with Him? Why do we pray before we eat? This helps us be grateful and see the goodness of God that is right before us. This helps us express the desires of the Holy Spirit within us. When we pray, we speak our desires that burn within us and then hope these desires are also God's desires.*

By gazing at *and* smelling *the goodness before us, our hearts are* touched, *and we continue to be grounded in our faith and stand on it. God is all that is* good *and* number one*! This is having a personal relationship with God because He is present everywhere with everyone.*

Days to Pentecost

50

After we celebrate the resurrection of Jesus, known as Easter, we then have fifty days until we celebrate the Holy Spirit's appearance with the twelve apostles. How well do we know these friends of Jesus so we can recognize the work we need to do in our life to spread the good news of my best friend, Jesus Christ? Do we have a relationship with the Holy Spirit daily? How could we improve this relationship?

Days in the Desert

40

Jesus spent forty days in the desert, talking to His Father. This was a lot of time in conversation and/or communication. Do we spend this amount of time in conversation and/or communication with our spiritual Father and/or with our physical father? Do we spend this amount of time in conversation with God on how we can be a better father or mother to our children or to the children in this world who seem not to have a good father figure and/or mother figure in their life who would help them discern the choices they make in their lives?

Days to Easter

40

    Our church sets aside forty special days for us to make choices on what kind of sacrifice or sting that we can live by to help us change into a better person. In forty days, after giving it a lot of work, we can be like a new person spiritually and as a family person or neighbor. We call this time Lent. Do we make sacrifices in our own lives for the good of others on a daily time line? How can we be intimate with our Lord and Savior if we are not in touch with the true meaning of sacrifice or love?

Books of the New Testament Bible

27

The ideal man and/or ideal woman lives his/her life reflecting the main teaching or value of each chapter of the New Testament. The Bible is the door to our faith. It is God speaking to us! Since the Bible is the blueprint in living before leaving earth, it is good to be knowledgeable on what it says on how to love and serve in this world. It is to become the language of our hearts. This Bible can be seen as a book of divine works and a book filled with blessings about life! The Bible is the best-selling book!

The main idea of each book of the Bible in the New Testament from my perspective is as follows:

THE GOSPELS
Matthew - Mission of Jesus

Knowing what Jesus's mission is allows us the opportunity to know Jesus better. So what was the mission of Jesus? What is the mission of Jesus?

In the beginning of the gospel of Matthew, we hear and learn about the genealogy of Jesus. Within this, we learn of the number fourteen. The total number of generations from Abraham to David is fourteen. The total number of generations from David to the Babylonian exile is fourteen. The total number of generations from the Babylonian exile to the Messiah is fourteen.

Mountains are often mentioned in the Bible. In chapter 5, Jesus goes up to the mountain and then preaches to His disciples. He teaches them how to live by teaching them the eight Beatitudes. This is also known as the sermon on the mount.

Then in chapter 6, we have Jesus teaching us how to pray: "Our Father in heaven, hallowed be Your name. Your kingdom come, Your will be done, on earth as it is in heaven. Give us today our daily bread, and forgive us our debts, as we forgive our debtors, and do not subject us to the final test, but deliver us from the evil one." If you forgive others their transgressions, your Heavenly Father will forgive you. But if you do not forgive others, neither will your Father forgive your transgressions.

Praying, as Jesus has taught us, will help us know the life He wants us to live. When we have times when we know that we need to pray because the world around us seems so confusing and people seem to be acting more like animals than people, do we pause and think and follow the example of Jesus and go to the mountain to talk to our God, the Father? Do we reflect often on the gospel of Matthew 8:1-5? This is only one of the several miracles performed by Jesus for the people!

Mark - Mystery of Jesus

This is the shortest of all the gospels, but it has some awesome stories of the miracles that Jesus performed. He performed numerous miracles at the time of His earthly presence and also today. This goes beyond our imagination. So many of them, we don't even know or realize! Wow!

John the Baptist proclaimed a baptism of repentance when he was in the desert. He baptized a lot of people in the Jordan River as they repented of their sins. He predicted and told them that One mightier would come and baptize with the Holy Spirit. Jesus also came and was baptized in the Jordan by John. At that moment, a voice came from heaven, saying, "You are My beloved Son. With You, I Am well pleased."

A lot of the miracles took place with some of His disciples with Him. As Jesus was going to many villages and teaching, He began to send the twelve apostles out two by two. He said to them, "Wherever you enter a house, stay there until you leave from there. Whatever place does not welcome you or listen to you, leave there and shake the dust off your feet in testimony against them." Many demons were cast out, and many people were cured.

The miracle of the feeding of the five thousand is quite well known by people. Being able to feed that many people from five loaves and two fish is certainly an amazing miracle!

How many other miracles did Jesus perform then? How many miracles are happening every day around us that we don't recognize or acknowledge? Have we read and reflected on this gospel? How long does it take? (For me, it is approximately eighty minutes, and this is about five minutes per chapter). Chapter 10 has good things on family life! In my senior religion class, we read and reflected on this gospel. It was primarily my first experience of studying the Bible in this way. This is a gift that I was given, and I am forever grateful for this part of my education!

Luke - Perspective of Jesus

Getting a simple and clear perspective of Jesus would come from these three facts: Jesus died, Jesus rose from the dead, and Jesus ascended into heaven.

In the gospel of Luke 23:44, we are given the description of the death of Jesus. From about noon until three in the afternoon, darkness came over the whole land. Then Jesus last words were "Father, into your hands I commend my spirit." Witnesses then said, "He was innocent beyond doubt."

At the beginning of chapter 24, we are given the description of the resurrection: At daybreak, on the first day of the week, they took the spices they had prepared and went to the tomb. They found the stone rolled away from the tomb, but when they entered, they did not find the body of the Lord Jesus. While they were puzzling over this, behold, two men in dazzling garments appeared to them. They were terrified and bowed their faces to the ground. They said to them, "Why do you seek the Living One among the dead? He is not here, but He has been raised. Remember what He said to you while He was still in Galilee, that the Son of Man must be handed over to sinners and be crucified and rise on the third day."

In chapter 24, beginning with the fiftieth verse, we are given the description of the ascension of Jesus: Then He led them out as far as Bethany, raised His hands, and blessed them. As He blessed them, He parted from them and was taken up to heaven. We have so many opportunities to go to church and receive blessings. Do we realize how good this is? Is it wrong or sinful to pass up these times to be loved?

In chapter 19, we have the story of Zacchaeus who was a tax collector and sinner. He was short, so I relate to this story! Jesus invited him to dinner. Are we partial to who we are with because of their size or their looks? Do we seek people with an attitude of hope? Do we have dinner with only certain people? Do we visit and communicate with sinners?

John - Signs of Jesus

The signs are also known as deeds. Jesus was a person doing deeds of love for others. This is a great model for all mankind. These signs are to help people become believers.

The wedding at Cana is a marvelous story of Jesus changing water into wine for the newly married couple and their guests. Jesus is being a caring person and is aware of the stress of people and responds with love.

The man born blind is brought to His attention by His disciples. The discussion arose about whose sin caused the blindness. Was it the man or the parents who sinned that cause the man to be blind? Jesus said that it was neither. Then He spat on the ground and made clay with the saliva and smeared the clay on the blind

9

man's eyes and said to him, "Go wash in the pool of Siloam." So the man went and washed and came back able to see.

The raising of Lazarus is another sign of the good deeds performed by Jesus. In Bethany, a man named Lazarus was ill. This was the brother of Mary and Martha. Mary was the one who had anointed the feet of Jesus with perfumed oil and dried them with her hair. They sent a message to Jesus that Lazarus was ill. Jesus decided to go to him, but the disciples discouraged Him because the Jews had tried to stone Him. When Jesus arrived, He found out that Lazarus had died and was in the tomb for four days. When Martha met Jesus, He told her, "Your brother will rise." Then they went to the tomb where Mary and the Jews were. There was a large crowd, and the Jews were carrying on about how Jesus cured the blind man and why didn't He help cure Lazarus. Then Jesus requested that the stone be taken away. They took away the stone and Jesus prayed. The dead man came out.

These are three of the wonderful signs and deeds of Jesus shared in the gospel! How much love did Jesus give to the people in His only three years of ministry? Are we ever like the Jews carrying on about how somebody did something or didn't do something without knowing the full story? For example, in my own history, probably few people know that I have participated in cleaning chicken barns, hog barns, and cattle barns. A few people probably know that I have hoed and picked many watermelons. If we don't fully know the whole story, we may not know why people act as they do. I am a strong believer in people having a "work ethic." Just ask any of my children!

Acts of the Apostles - Entertaining Events

This is a lot about events that took place when the apostles and other disciples went out teaching and preaching about Jesus to many people in many countries. The events that took place while doing this were not always fun, but they were action-filled which can explain why they may have been seen as entertaining.

We first learn about some of the preparation that went on for these mission journeys. The apostles needed to replace Judas, so they did that. Then they spent time with one another and the Holy Spirit in prayer to be able to be in touch on how they were going to preach and teach.

The mission work that was done in so many countries and towns to let people know who our Lord and Savior, Jesus Christ, is work that is so fantastic. Some of these places are Jerusalem, Judea, Samaria, Ethiopia, Damascus, Lydda, Antioch, Cyprus, Pamphylia, Iconium, Lystra, Lycaonia, Asia Minor, Macedonia, Europe, Philippi, Thessalonica, Beroea, Athens, Areopagus, Corinth, Ephesus, Greece, Miletus, Assos, Mitylene, Samos, Tyre, Ptolemais, Caesarea, Rome, and Malta.

Some of the people involved in the events of the mission work were Peter, the apostles, Stephen, Saul, Philip, Simon, Cornelius, the Gentiles, the crippled beggar, the Ethiopian, Agabus, Herod, Barnabas, Symeon, Lucius, Manaen, Timothy, James, Felix, Caesar, King Agrippa, and the Jews. The numerous events and people involved in spreading the good news of Jesus Christ is so out of the ordinary and so inspiring!

Some of the events to reflect on were the promises of the Spirit; the Ascension; the first community of Jerusalem; the choice of Judas's successor; the coming of the Spirit; Peter's speech; the communal life; when the crippled beggar was cured; the Sanhedrin; the prayer of the community; life in the Christian community; the signs and wonders of the apostles; the need for assistants; the accusations against Stephen; Stephen's discourse; Stephen's martyrdom; Saul's conversion; Saul's baptism; Saul's preaching; Saul's visit to Jerusalem; Peter's healing; Peter's life restoration; Cornelius's vision; Peter's vision; Cornelius's baptism; baptisms of the Gentiles; the church at Antioch; Herod's persecution of the Christians; Herod's death; the mission of Barnabas and Saul; Paul's arrival at Antioch; Paul's address in the synagogue; Paul's address to the Gentiles; the council of Jerusalem; James on the dietary law; the letter of the apostles; the delegates at Antioch; Paul and Barnabas's separation, imprisonment, and deliverance from Prison; Paul's journeys; Paul's speech; the riot of the silversmiths; Paul's farewell speech; Paul's arrest; Paul's defense; Paul's imprisonment; reactions to Paul's speech; and Paul's departure for Rome, storm and shipwreck, arrival in Rome, and testimony to Jews in Rome.

Those are places and people and events so numerous and filled with meaning! There is so much to learn and understand! What inspiring and entertaining event or events can one create that reflects the gospel message? What entertaining and inspiring events are on our calendar or in our schedule? All this also seems like a lot of work and sacrificing! Wow!

NEW TESTAMENT LETTERS
Romans - Faith in Christ

Paul was a disciple and a slave for Christ Jesus. He became an ideal man following the greatest ideal man, Jesus Christ.

As Paul writes and teaches, "The one who is righteous by faith will live." We need to live the gospel. Idolaters are to be punished, but God is the One who is the just judge.

Justification comes from Jesus Christ because God has been manifested apart from the law. Abraham believed in God and, because of his righteousness, inherited faith. He was empowered by faith and gave glory to God. Having faith in God gives us peace. With the endurance of our afflictions, hope is produced. While we were sinners, Christ died for us, proving His love for us.

Knowing the duties of a Christian, life is a process of discerning what God wants us to do. We ask and search our minds and hearts reflecting, asking ourselves, what is good and pleasing and perfect? Are we living and dying for Christ? Do I need one dog (Lassie and/or Spot) or one cat (Blackie and/or Smokey) to be able to do this? Does it need to be inside or outside? Do I need to spend every day responding to its needs? In the small things we do every day, are they perfect and pleasing to God?

Are we about the salvation of our own soul and the salvation of all souls of the world? How are we doing with this? This letter of Paul's to the Romans is the longest of his letters.

1 Corinthians - Need to Help the Less Fortunate

This letter is primarily written to the Gentiles who ignore the law. They were worshipping all kinds of gods and causing disunity in the community. Corinth is a seaport city located on the narrow midsection of Greece.

Paul is referred to as an apostle for Jesus. He spent his days teaching and preaching on divisions within the church that need not be and how ministers are to conduct themselves. Teaching on sexuality, incest, and lawsuits was of great concern. How in touch are we with these kinds of moral disorders of today? What are we doing about it? Do we know the numbers in our town and/or county? Why not? Do we cover up immoral acts? Do we avoid getting the truth and expect others to do the right thing too?

Paul gives a lot of advice to the married, the widows, and the virgins. He preaches how we all need to seek the good of the other. He has a lot to say on what love is! This is in chapter 13. Do we know what all he has to say? With his exceptional insight on what love is, we also hear the use of gifts of each individual.

For instance, in today's world, the hardest issue for a couple to deal with is finances. It is one of the top reasons for divorce and/or conflict. It is so important in family relationships that the one most skilled in the area of finances needs to do them and be a leader of them. The other spouse needs to give them their support. No secret agendas are necessary in order for the needs of the household to be taken care of. A certain amount of freedom needs to be allowed in order not to crush the spirit of the others' gifts once the needs are being met. A good explanation of the gifts of others is in chapter 12.

Many people do not know the seriousness of sins and need to be taught. Feeling like the mean guy just might be what God is expecting us to do. The lukewarm and carefree attitude is not the right one. We all need to build one another up, the natural body and the spiritual one, especially the less fortunate.

This is an extensive and serious letter.

2 Corinthians - The Role of Each One's Cross

We begin with the awareness again of Paul as an apostle. Many people turned Paul's followers away. There became a crisis between Paul and the Corinthians.
There was a lot of controversy. How do we handle controversy in our relationships with others? Do we ignore things that shouldn't be? Are we good listeners and respond in love when controversy arises?

Galatians - Share the Gifts of the Spirit

This is a harsh letter but one with passion. It is also seen as a somewhat of an autobiography of Paul. He is known as the uncharitable and radical Paul with the Galatians. These Gentiles kept the law. Highlights of this letter are Paul establishing credibility, the importance of faith over the law, freedom to love your neighbor, and the inclusion of women. Do we let the gifts of the Spirit shine through by being a person who people can believe because of your dependable and honest character? Do we recognize the importance of our faith? Do we love others in the way God wants us to? Do we include and listen to women when we make decisions about work, family, and church?
This letter does not have the message of thanksgiving like the majority of Paul's letters.

Ephesians - A Call to Unity

This letter is more of an essay. Paul is concerned with relationship between the Jews and Gentiles. The theme is a call to unity. Our unity as a church and a people are called upon as presented in the seven unities of the church: one baptism, one church, one faith, one God and Father of all, one hope, one Lord, and one Spirit. This is in Ephesians 4:4-6.
We learn a lot on exhortations based on the union with Christ, exhortations to household duties, and final exhortations. How much energy and education do we put into our family unity and oneness? How united and one is our domestic family? How united in oneness are married couples?

Philippians - Enthusiasm and Rejoicing

Paul wrote this letter from prison. Philippi was a city located in Northern Greece. He expected these people to stay strong in faith and get ready for the end of time. During this time, these people believed in magic. The theme for this letter is a call to sharing a life of service.

Let us reflect and ponder on these verses of service to the world: "For God is the one who, for His good purpose, works in you both to desire and to work. Do everything without grumbling or questioning, that you may be blameless and innocent, children of God without blemish in the midst of a crooked and perverse generation." This scripture passage is in the Liturgy of the Hours. (This verse reminds me of shows and comments as the "grumpy old man" is portrayed!) Of course, all humans have moments of being grumpy! What do we do with our time to make this a better world for all people? Do we live the words of these verses in our daily life? Do we have an attitude of rejoicing and have a heart of enthusiasm in our daily service to God's people?

Colossians - Virtues and Vices

This letter is primarily filled with virtues and vices. There continues to be that concern for the relationships between the Jews and the Gentiles. This letter also is calling people to unity like in the letter to the Ephesians. How well educated are we on the difference of virtues and vices? Do we make our decisions based on them, or do we just go with the crowd or just do whatever someone asks us to without praying and reflecting on it being a virtue or a vice?

1 Thessalonians - Joy, Thanksgiving, and Hope

This letter is written from Corinth and is one of the earliest writings. Thessalonica is another seaport city in Northern Greece. It is a letter of joy and thanksgiving. The theme is to live in the world in love with the faith that Christ has already been raised from the dead and in the hope that He will soon return to establish God's kingdom. Exhortations of good behavior are in 1 Thessalonians 5:12-22.

What are some of my moments of joy and thanksgiving? Do they just happen? Do I make sacrifices and do good deeds and then have these moments of joy and thanksgiving that just happen?

2 Thessalonians - Live a Model Lifestyle

This letter implies that persecution has increased and that the day of the Lord has come. The theme or message is to live in accord with the Jesus story. How much research do we do to find a model lifestyle? Are we people who just float through life without really digging in order to give it thought and meaning? Do we see a model lifestyle as a life of pleasure-filled moments for myself, like the squirrels running up and down tree branches and the scampering across the field? Who do we know personally that we see as someone who is living a model lifestyle? What are the qualities they have?

1 Timothy - Teachings and Worship

This is a personal letter in which orders of teaching and worship are contained. There are also warnings about heresy. What does heresy mean? To me, heresy is a lie about my religious beliefs. Sometimes people say things as if it is a church teaching, and it is not correct. To me, this is dishonesty. Sometimes it could be from not being educated in that area of religion. People who worship with their heart and then respond by doing good things from their best understanding are people we want to learn from. These people are living the truth! They are not hypocrites. Sometimes, during worship, it seems hard to be engaged fully and not be distracted. This is an area that I need to continuously work on and try to stay focused and connected.

2 Timothy - Stand by the Truth

This is a personal letter with pieces of advice: to stand by the truth, proclaim the gospel message, know that the last days are evil, and remember Christ. Do we ever find it hard to stand by the truth? Do we just go along with things without making the truthful stands that we should for things to be right? Sometimes it can be a real challenge when working with people who are so negative that one just wants to lie and agree with them on their issue because that seems to be the easier and comfortable thing to do. Sometimes I avoid vocal people because I often conclude that they don't listen to a word I say and I am wasting my time. This may be true, but I need not wimp out and avoid what should be known and stated.

Titus - Christian Behavior

This is a personal letter that contains a treatment for heretics. What could be a treatment for heretics? All are to do good works and treat others with generous love. Do we pray about what kind of Christian behavior we are portraying each day? Do we recognize actions or words of Christians that are heretic? Do we make efforts to teach what is right?

Philemon - Freedom and Partnership

This letter was written from prison. It is a story of freedom and partnership in a new community. It is a short letter to a slave owner in which Paul asks that his friend be freed to work with him. Do we appreciate our freedom to worship?

Are we like those squirrels that seem so free and full of energy in their work and play? Do we see our faith that way, or do we selfishly cling to it as if it belongs to ourselves? We could be like those squirrels living with an attitude of gratitude of being free and full of energy to share our love for God by inviting others in faith activities of work or faith activities of play!

Hebrews - Priestly Service

This is a letter primarily focused on the establishment of Jesus's priestly service and the implications of that service for life and worship. The introduction and conclusion center on the superiority of Jesus. We are given the advice to pay attention to our behavior and act like we believe. We are to draw near to God and live a life of holiness. Does one's service to others have a high level of personal communication? Do we invite and come to know all the people in our church community? Are we partial to those who come to the worship services and not even come to know those who don't? I was so inspired by a story recently on television of a priest walking the streets to greet the people of his town and at the same time praying! I have a few memories of a priest inviting my husband and I to a home-cooked meal. In the Bible, there are times when Jesus shared a meal with someone. This is definitely an example of priestly service. This is also what all baptized Christians are called to do. My mom was so great at this kind of thing. She was a person with great hospitality filled with enthusiasm! Who are other people who model this virtue?

A lot of the New Testaments letters contain "greetings" to people. They also contain "messages of thanks." What an example of the virtues of hospitality, generosity, and a grateful heart!

CATHOLIC LETTERS
James - Ethical Conduct

This letter was written in the first century and is a Greek letter. It was probably written by James or one who was inspired by him. It is more like an essay dressed up like a letter on morality. The teaching is on the role of faith to continue living a steadfast life.

Faith is dead without works. With this, we are to strive with patience, truthfulness, prayer, and the rescue of those who wander. What is faith in action? Is this being seen clearly of being more important than the words we speak? It is so inspiring to see someone living what they teach and preach! These people are heroes and people to be so grateful for!

1 Peter - The Gift of Baptism

The theme of this writing is of suffering. The setting is in the Christian communities of Roman Asia Minor. This is the only work contributed to Peter because it seems that Peter would have been the one to write advice on baptism. The blessing on the newborn is precious and inspiring. The blessing that is given to parents who are nourishing their unborn baby is a practice that is precious and inspiring! This blessing has not been as obvious in our churches as days past. I hope these blessings will be done for all babies! This letter contains advice on lifestyles, conduct, duties of the servants, sufferings, baptism, wives, husbands, and everyone.

2 Peter - Positive Instructions

This letter is addressed to the Gentiles with a concern for them which consists of general instructions and warnings. The basic concern of the writer is a vision of baptism.

There is advice about false teachers, scoffers, and behavior. Do we stop to think about what kind of positive instructions we can give in our daily lives in our relationships with others? Wouldn't this help in making sure we make better decisions and be better at recognizing false teachers and false or bad behavior?

1 John - Jesus became Man

The main theme is that Jesus Christ became man. (This is the incarnation.) It contains warnings about the anti-Christ. It also teaches the marks of God's children. These are not committing sin, loving one another, keeping Jesus's word, believing that Jesus became man and having the spirit of love. What are some anti-Christ actions? Do we recognize them?

2 John - Love and Trust

The main theme is love and trust. It also brings out the need to be aware of deceivers. Do we spend time in prayer asking the Holy Spirit to help us recognize and be aware of the deceivers in our day-to-day communications? Do we just trust in anybody and anything? By asking for the help of the Holy Spirit, we can better put our love and trust to work where it needs to be.

3 John - Hospitality

The main theme is hospitality. It also teaches on condemnation of strangers and condemnation of those we do not receive as our brothers and sisters in our human family. Being hospitable helps us not to condemn others. Do we reflect on the fact that being hospitable and kind is not the same as going along with whatever someone presents us?

Jude - Become Holy

This writing is more of a sermon than a letter. The three main teachings are to fight for the faith, make the scriptures known, and give advice to the faithful. How can we make the scriptures known if we don't participate in Bible studies? How can we make scripture known if we don't invite and encourage others to participate in Bible studies? How can we make scripture known if we are not studying it ourselves? How can we make scripture known when most people who attend or don't attend Mass do not even think enough to realize the Bible readings from the Old Testament and New Testament are proclaimed daily and more often?

Six years ago, when my granddaughter was born and she stayed in the hospital for seven weeks, I spent a lot of time writing a simple Bible study that includes games for the young and adults. Some of the youth have participated in it since then and are reading and studying the New Testament for the second time! I don't understand why adults refuse to participate, except for those who have difficulty understanding the language. I don't understand why clergy don't support it and promote it more. I don't understand why I, myself, have not promoted it more.

Revelation - Hope for Righteousness

This is a letter filled with the writer's hope and conviction that God would soon overthrow evil and establish a new age of righteousness. It is a story with imagination.

It opens with a reference to the seven churches, then the vision "in the spirit of the Lord's Day," we have "the letter scroll," "the heavenly Scroll," and "the scroll of the heavens."

COVID-19 is a true revelation of the meaning of pro-life. What actions are being taken to promote life? What rules are not respected in support of the true meaning and value of life?

Have you ever been fascinated with the imagination of a child? Do we work at letting our imagination with God as our partner go to work in our daily lives? Like, oh, another day of adventure here on earth, so what can I best create or do for You, my God?

The Bible is the inspired word of God, and it is also known as sacred scripture. This book is the best sold book around! Could we learn enough from reading and reflecting on the messages available to guide us and give us comfort in living each day of our lives? Opportunities of learning, hoping, and loving are so available for us! It delights God when we make our home with one another! How well do we listen? Do we search for God? Do we yearn for God? Do we desire God? Do we have a relationship with the word of God that lifts us with a great mission before us? Do we rejoice in His strength? Do we see the Bible as a tabernacle? What is a tabernacle? A tabernacle represents God's presence.

When we need to be healed, do we consume the word? When we need to be healed, do we consume the Eucharist?

The Stations of the Cross

14

The ideal man and/or ideal woman makes the sacrifices needed to have a good family life, religious life, priest ministry, or single life. Reading and reflecting and responding to the sacrifices Jesus made for us can only deepen our daily commitment to live each day in gratitude for His love.

1. Jesus is condemned to death.

Pilate condemned Jesus. He did not know Him personally. How was Mary, His mother, feeling when she heard the people around shouting, "Crucify Him"? Do we condemn others or pass judgment on others we do not know personally or completely? Let us respond with a commitment to accept the difficult times in our life.

2. The Lord carries His cross.

Jesus was made to carry the cross by the soldiers, while people cursed and made fun of Him. How did Mary, His mother, feel when she saw Him stumble out and was given the heavy wooden cross to carry? Do we have crosses that we bear in order to make this world a better place to live in? Let us respond by not being envious of the wrongdoing of others.

3. Jesus falls the first time.

Jesus was too weak to carry the cross, so he fell while people cheered His weakness. Was Mary filled with trembling as she watched her Son kicked, whipped, and fell with the cross? Do we ever feel heavy demands by others on us and not carry our load well? Do we lack the patience and strength that we need in our life? Let us respond by recognizing our weaknesses of sin and change our ways.

4. Jesus meets His sorrowful mother.

Mary wanted the best for Jesus. She wanted Him to be liked by others. He came to appear to be a public failure in the eyes of a lot of people who did not know the real story of Jesus. When Mary, with tears in her eyes, looked at Jesus, she knew that she had to take courage because of the purpose of this sacrifice. Do we feel like Mary when others fail to see the true story of who we are, what we do, and what our purpose is? Let us respond by having the courage to look our mother in the eye when we know that we could do better.

5. Simon helps Jesus carry the cross.

Simon helped Jesus carry the cross. But did he really want to? Was he a reluctant person? Are we reluctant to follow Jesus and carry our cross? Mary was silent. She obeyed and followed Jesus. Is this what we do? Let us respond with hearts of generosity and kindness to those we meet each day.

6. Veronica wipes the face of Jesus.

Veronica took the extra step to comfort Jesus. Mary watched and knew why she was doing this. Do we take extra steps to care for others? Do we focus more on the needs of others rather than ourselves? Do we miss a lot of opportunities to give to others each day? Let us respond by reflecting on the most recent opportunities that we missed to give to others.

7. Jesus falls the second time.

Jesus was weighed down by the weight of the cross and fell a second time. There was no one there who came up to help him. How was Mary, His mother, feeling at this time as she saw Him fall a second time as He was carrying the cross? Do we ever feel weighted down by our duties and responsibilities? Do we relate to Jesus at these times, pick ourselves up, and move forward? Let us respond to others with empathy and recognize them when they are carrying a cross.

8. Jesus meets the women of Jerusalem.

When Jesus met the women crying and weeping, they seemed to be weeping for themselves. How did Mary feel when she saw the women of Jerusalem shedding tears and then Jesus telling them to shed tears for their conversion and not for Him? Do we weep for others, or do we weep because we have failed to share the love and truth of Jesus? Do we blame others and weep for ourselves, or do we continue to follow our calling and commitment? Let us respond with sincere hearts for all women who are experiencing challenges.

9. Jesus falls the third time.

Jesus fell again as the soldiers and crowd just watched. How did Mary feel as she saw her son fell on rocky ground while being screamed at and then seeing Him being dragged on the ground? When we fall or when we see others fall, do we respond with a humble heart? Do we take courage to help others and ask others to help us? Let us respond with a persistent love when we see the need.

10. Our Lord is stripped of His garments.

Everything was taken from Jesus. He was made helpless and so disrespected. He had given so much to others, and now this was how he was treated. How did Mary feel seeing the terrible pain of her Son without any chance to rest? When we feel that everything is being taken away from us, how do we respond? How do we keep giving when we long for a little praise or a little sign of thanks? Let us respond by helping those who give so much of their time and talents to others. In today's world, this is being called bullied. How much do we know concerning this issue with our young people? Is bullying someone in our domestic homes done and accepted as being an okay thing to do?

11. Jesus is nailed to the cross.

Jesus was physically abused with shoving and throwing and then nailed to the cross. As they nailed Him to the cross, what kind of feelings would Mary be feeling? How do we feel when we give so much to others and it is not acknowledged and when we are criticized for things not in our control? How do we deal with times of being blamed falsely for things? Let us respond with action to stop the abuse in this world.

12. Our Lord dies on the cross.

Dying on the cross was pain endured by Jesus. The physical and mental pain was beyond our imagination. He listened to the call of His Father and followed it. He served others by teaching, going without rest, going without food and water, and now enduring pain. How can His mother endure the pain as she watches her

Son in that pain? Do we ever wonder where the people are who we have sacrificed and agonized over when we endure pain? Do we ever wonder if we are making a difference for others? Let us try to respond to others by teaching them the right way to help others who are in pain.

13. Jesus is taken down from the cross.

When Jesus was taken down from the cross, He was put in the arms of His mother. How sad she must have felt with all the blood, dirt, and sweat, but because she knew this had to be, she prayed silently. Do we hold out our arms for others with love? Do we have this kind of unconditional love for others? Let us respond by helping people with their dark moments by listening and helping them see a new light for their life.

14. Jesus is laid in the sepulcher (tomb).

Jesus was placed in a tomb that did not belong to Him. It was the tomb for Joseph of Arimathea. Since Mary knew all this had to be, she waited in faith. Jesus was buried with dignity. Do we live as nothing belongs to us? Do we seek things that Jesus never did? Do we truly believe that God's reward is enough for us? Let us respond by always keeping in mind that nothing belongs to us.

THE RESURRECTION

Jesus offers us the promise of resurrection, so let us continue to give ourselves for others. Let us live in the hope of that day for our Lord to say, "Well done, my good and faithful servant, welcome to my kingdom." Truly, Jesus is the ideal man. Truly, Mary is the ideal woman.

My most touching experience of the Stations of the Cross was led by a deacon who truly made it seem like I was at the passion of Christ and in the space of Mary Magdalene and Mary, the mother of Jesus. This happened over twenty-five years ago. This deacon is now a priest, and I hope and pray that he is still maintaining that very obvious closeness and connection with Jesus.

Works of Mercy

14

The ideal man and/or woman know all seven spiritual works of mercy and all seven corporal works of mercy because he/she continuously do them. The best inspirations for me about the works of mercy are through the actions and conversations of children. It is so true that the Lord would teach us that we cannot enter the kingdom of heaven unless we become like the little children!

Corporal Works of Mercy
Feed the Hungry

Who is so willing to share their food with others? So often a baby is not even one year old and he/she is feeding mom or dad part of their food. The children in elementary school love to share their food with their friends and bring treats and food to their teachers, especially on holidays! Do we, as adults, share food by giving to others in need? Do we work at the food pantry or help take meals to homes when needed?

Give Drink to the Thirsty

This is not talking about Peach Crown Royal or Bud Light! Primarily, this can be with a different meaning, like letting someone know who Jesus is because they need the life and love that comes from knowing and encountering Jesus. I have experienced a lot of children who have invited their friends to come and read the Bible with them but then are rejected. I have experienced youth inviting their friends to come to a retreat, and then they are rejected. Do we know the young people in our church community enough to know about these experiences they are having when they reach out to share the gospel messages with others? We can give drink to the thirsty by paying attention and recognizing any person of any age and responding to them with support or an invitation. If we have a close relationship with Jesus, we will find ourselves thirsting for Him.

Shelter the Homeless

It has been so inspiring and interesting to hear children share how they were in a big city and seen homeless people on the street with a sign. They were so proud to tell the story of how their mom and/or dad gave money to those homeless people.

Clothe the Naked

Some people in our own towns and cities do not have proper clothes to wear because they don't have money to buy them. Some people just don't know what clothes are proper to buy and wear and need to be taught the what and why of clothes. If a younger brother or sister is cold, a response of sharing with those in need comes so willingly from most children. They just seem to know the good thing to do. Are we learning a lot from the actions of children in this world? How can we become like them if we are not in tune with their innocence, love, and imagination?

Visit Those in Prison

Some people are in their own prison and don't even know they are and why they are. They just feel alone and unloved. Children often respond so lovingly when there is a new student at school and go out of their way to invite them into play and talk to them.

Sometimes we hesitate to think about and pray for those in prison. Sometimes we are not allowed to visit those in prison or they prefer not to see us. This is acceptable and not a reason to ignore their memories or to cease having them in our prayers. Do we pray for anyone in prison? Do we pray for those people we know that should be in prison for their immoral actions?

Visit the Sick

It is so good to see children help one another when one gets injured. They tend to have a compassion that you do not always see in most adults. When their mom is pregnant, they often tell stories on how they help out in many ways in their homes. This is not implying that a pregnant woman is sick. She has a special condition of challenges going on that she needs to accept and deal with as she daily promotes the breath and life of two people. As adults, do we truly give the support to these women as they deserve? Do we speak pro-life and then not truly live it? Do we truly know what it is to be pro-life in all aspects?

Bury the Dead

I have been the most inspired by the Native American burials where family and friends participate by covering the casket with dirt. There is a sense of respect and unity with their loved one at this time. What kind of respect do we have for those who have died? Do we remember them in our prayers? Do we share beliefs about death with others?

Spiritual Works of Mercy
Instruct the Ignorant

There is so much wisdom that comes out of the mouths of young children. Not only a sense of wisdom, but also a profound sense of the reality and truth is shared by them. For example, when a parent takes a picture of their child with a sport jersey shirt on from the front side and then asks to take the back side of the name, while another child says, giggling, "So now do you want to take a picture of our butts?"

Another comment from a teenager might be, "Why do I need to do worksheets and other papers when I can just do my own studying and ace the test? Why do I get bad grades because I choose not to waste time?" Sometimes we see young children and youth as ignorant, when, in reality, they have some serious messages of truth. There is so much that we don't know and need to strive to learn. Some of it comes from education, and some of it comes from experiences. Do we listen carefully to the experiences of others so we get what they are doing or saying?

Counsel the Doubtful

Have you ever experienced an "I can't child"? This is a child who responds often with those words, and it is more of a lack of confidence than not being able to do something. Rather, be it a child or an adult, we all need encouragement and people in our lives who believe in us. The apostle Saint Thomas was definitely an example of this because he needed proof so he could believe that Jesus had died on the cross. Do we believe because we have reason to believe, or do we believe because it makes me feel good or makes me feel important?

Admonish the Sinner

Children are great at letting their elder or younger brother or sister know if they are not doing right. They are especially good at telling their parents about what the other one did or is doing. In school, classmates are often very good at telling on one another. Sometimes even very young children (preschoolers) will tell their parents if their teenage brother and/or sister have a party when the parents are gone for the evening. Are we people who go along with the sins of others? Are we like children who speak the truth?

Bear Wrongs with Patience

Have you ever told a child that you are sorry? They are the fastest and most sincere with their response. Have you ever seen or experienced their patience with younger children or the elderly? Sometimes one sees a child just waiting patiently for their parent to get done talking with someone or watch their eyes when they look at their parent with that look of hope for their parent to just quit drinking or smoking. What innocent examples of bearing wrong with patience do you observe in others? What kind of response do we give when we experience this inspiration?

Forgive Injuries

Just two days ago, one middle school child was blaming the other and vice versa. When they were asked what they should do about their actions, they both immediately said, "I am sorry," and the disturbance ceased. I was quite shocked about their forgiving each other in such a good manner and so quickly. They truly seemed sincere. How truly sorry are we when we do wrong? Do we reflect on how we can make this not happen in the first place so I am not putting myself in a position of needing to be sorry?

Comfort the Sorrowful

Just yesterday, a five-year-old was hurt from running across the parking lot and then falling down. His knee got hurt on the concrete. In a quick second, a half dozen children were gathered there to help and called for an adult. He had scraped his knee, but their help to get him a Band-Aid and be with him continued. Is this the way adults respond when someone needs to be comforted?

27

Pray for the Living and the Dead

I have heard children pray for other small children who are in the hospital. It is so precious because of the concern and compassion that come through their voices. They often have an eagerness to do more, like make get-well cards for the child and then cards for the parents. Have you ever heard teenagers pray for a grandma or grandpa who just died? Sometimes we think teenagers don't have a heart, but so many of them do.

The most generous, helpful people I have ever met have been children. Adults may help a person, but when a youth or a child helps out, they often have an enthusiasm that makes one feel grateful you asked them. They seem to be generous because it is a kind deed from their heart and not from a sense of obligation or because they think they "have to." Children seem to be so genuine. The scripture passage that says that we need to become like children in order to enter the kingdom has become so believable to me. I feel so blessed to have had so many experiences of the true, real-life love of children!

The Last Supper

The Last Supper was not only a wow *moment, but also a precious gift for all mankind! Jesus, the real ideal man, shared a meal with his twelve friends, the apostles. This meal continues over two thousand years later all over the world! What kind of a* wow *is that?*

The Apostles

12

The ideal man and/or woman knows who the twelve apostles are and what was their strong virtue in living their life for God. Tradition tells us a lot about these men. These are the famous heroes of Jesus to follow:

Andrew

Andrew was the first apostle to hear Christ's call and followed Him. He was a fisherman. He took his elder brother, Peter, to meet Him, and he followed Jesus too. He preached the message of Jesus in Greece, Turkey, and Russia. He was martyred because he refused to worship a pagan god. Andrew was known to be the first friend of Jesus. He was a gentleman, doing everything with love and gentleness.

Bartholomew

Bartholomew was one of the twelve apostles. His name means "son of thunder." He is also known as Nathaniel. He studied the law and prophets. This apostle studied the Bible under the fig tree. He was Jewish and preached in Turkey, Asia Minor, and Arabia. He died a martyr in Armenia, where his skin was cut from his body. He was known as a person with creativity and vision. Spiritual ideas came through him and his teachings.

James the Greater

James the Greater was one of twelve apostles and the elder brother of John, the evangelist. He was a fisherman, and he and his brother followed Jesus. He preached in Samaria, Judea, and Spain. He was the first apostle to die for Christ. He died when he was killed with a sword from the order of King Herod in the year 43. He is known to be the first apostle to go on a missionary journey. He lived with good judgment and was a man showing discernment in his work.

James the Less

James the Less was a cousin of Jesus and a brother of the apostle Jude. He was called to be an apostle after the other James so that is why he is called James the Less. He was the bishop of Jerusalem and was known to have prayed so hard that his knees became as hard as a camel's. He died a martyr at the age of eighty-six, when he was flung from a tower for honoring Christ as the Son of God. He prayed for many hours in the temple and was responsible for many converts. A dream and a hope for the people of today is to see people praying for many hours in the temple! What joy all people could experience if this was true in churches today!

John

John was the youngest of the apostles, a fisherman, and a follower of Jesus. He is the brother of James the Greater. He was also known as a "son of thunder." He preached in Samaria and Palestine with Peter. He wrote the fourth gospel containing so many "signs of love." He was a prisoner in Rome and thrown into a pot of boiling water, but God kept him safe. In the year 100, he died a martyr in Ephesus. He was with Jesus at a lot of significant events. He was at the foot of the cross when Jesus entrusted His mother, Mary, to him. He was known as the beloved disciple.

Jude

Jude was a brother of the apostle James the Less. He preached in Arabia with the apostle Simon and then preached in Persia where he died for his faith. He was killed in the year 100 after being beaten to death with a club and then beheaded. He was also known as Thaddeus. Today he is known as the patron saint of hopeless cases. We have St. Jude's Hospital to help us be aware of the sick times that people are experiencing and the hope for better days to come.

Matthew

Matthew was a tax collector but was called to be an apostle to follow Jesus. A lot of Jews were angry because Jesus had asked him to follow Him. Tax collectors were known to be people who cheated others. Matthew was seen as a sinner, but Jesus told them, "I have come not to call the just but the sinners." He preached in Greece, Persia, and Syria. The gospel of Matthew was written in Aramaic for the Jewish converts. He was a man who worked to surrender to God's will and not to human will.

Matthias

Matthias became the twelfth apostle because he took the place of Judas. This was done as directed by Peter and because twelve was a special number of the Israelite people. There were twelve tribes of Israel. There were twelve patriarchs. Then this made twelve apostles for the New Israel. He preached in Ethiopia and Judea. He was martyred by being stoned to death in the year 64. He was the one present at the baptism of Jesus by John the Baptist and also at the resurrection of Jesus.

Peter, the First Pope

Peter was a fisherman, and Andrew was his brother. He denied Jesus three times but then repented. He was the first pope of the church and was known as one who ruled kindly and worked many miracles. He preached in Jerusalem, Antioch, and Rome. He died in Rome and was crucified upside down on a cross. Peter is mentioned 195 times in the New Testament. He was an inspired leader of not only the apostles, but also for the seventy disciples set forth by Jesus to preach, teach, and perform miracles.

Phillip

Phillip was one of the apostles who followed Jesus and had his best friend, Bartholomew, follow Jesus too. He brought people from Greece to hear Jesus's teaching. He preached in Turkey and Asia Minor. He was crucified in Phrygia. Philip was with Jesus at the feeding of the five thousand people. He was a practical and down-to-earth man.

Simon

Simon was a follower of Jesus. He was called the zealot because he belonged to a group that worked to keep the patriotic spirit of the Jews. He preached in Arabia and Persia with Jude. He was martyred by being cut in half with a saw. He and his brother Jude refused to worship false gods, so they were put to death.

Because of his association with Jesus, Simon became gentle and loving to others, and he dedicated his life to the ministry of the gospel.

Thomas

Thomas was the apostle who followed Jesus but struggled to believe in Him. He was a doubter but changed his life and became a strong believer. He preached in Persia, India, and Parthia. He was martyred in Parthia. Thomas was the one who risked his life and went with Jesus to visit Lazarus when he was sick. It is said that he built a church with his own hands in East India.

The apostles were friends of Jesus and His servants. Their lives of love, sacrifice, and good deeds are filled with much to learn from in order to be a true follower of Jesus!

The Fruits of the Holy Spirit

12

In order to be an ideal man and/or woman, one knows what it is that is important in order to be fruitful for others. We are all called to the freedom of service. We strive to share the Fruits of the Holy Spirit with others in our life and in our day-to-day events. A review of these or a new or different way of reflecting on these is as follows:

Charity

Charity is giving of oneself voluntarily to help others. This may be by giving money or sharing one's resources with others. It may be by good actions to help others physically, intellectually, emotionally, or spiritually. Physically, people who work in food pantries or serve in kitchens to help those in need are doing charitable work. People who encourage others in time of need like birthright volunteers are helping people in their emotional state of life. Anyone who encourages or compliments another's good works is living the model of charity. Whenever one shares their knowledge of anything for the good of another is promoting the intellectual well-being of another, an act of charity. The many spiritual leaders of churches and family leaders in a home that promote the spiritual life on a daily basis are people of charity. People who see their life as primarily a "gift" and not as a "right" have an attitude of charity that is on their mind and in their heart.

Joy

Joy is what nourishes our soul when life is difficult. It is when one endures his or her crosses in a loving way. When one bears the hardships in their life for the good of others, this is joy. When a parent cares for their sick child or loved one, there can be a joy at the conclusion of this difficult time. When one loses their job or a self-employed business, there can be joy when a new way is found.

Peace

Peace is a sense of being calm, quiet, and having the freedom from disturbances or the freedom from distractions. I have witnessed so many priests who pray with their whole heart and then radiate this peace in their faces like during and after the celebration of Mass or after they have spent a lot of time in adoration at church. My heart yearns for more leaders of the church, especially clergy, to be seen as people deeply connected with God by their many hours in church praying. Churches seem so empty these days compared to when I was a child and a teenager. I remember the days when priests were seen praying before Mass, after Mass, and a lot of other times. Their purpose in life was so obvious, and it was so inspiring. Married people and single people seemed to be in church praying almost at any time of the day as well. Could everyone make an effort to be more of a model of peace and quiet and have a visible union with God? I need to exert more effort too.

Patience

Patience is having an inner respect for time because they decide to control their emotions. A lot of people who practice having peace in their every moment of life also have a higher level of patience.

Nurses and doctors practice patience in their dealings with ill people because this is when they share their emotions from not feeling well, also teachers who work day in and day out with children who are in a confused and stress-filled home. Often these children respond to teachers with no patience. This takes a teacher's response at a high level of patience to help children work through their confusions and their lack of feeling loved or self-worth.

I, myself, find that I need to spend a lot more time in prayer and being connected with God so that I have more patience with others. I have very little patience with adults who don't listen and with adults who act like a kid who doesn't know the meaning of the word respect yet because of their actions. A lack of thanks is extremely irritating to me as well as being treated like an unvalued woman.

Benignity (Kindness)

Kindness is being friendly and generous. This is the work of people in clothing stores and places like Wal-Mart. Being a cashier or a people greeter in a store takes a person doing several kind acts, greeting them, being of service for them, and thanking them. Sometimes this is being done because of obligations for their own family's survival. Sometimes people are very rude, but one tries to kill them with kindness just to get through the workday. This is just the best thing to do because no one ever knows what the other person is going through in their life. How kind are we when we are shopping? Do we hoard and stock up on things? At the time of COVID-19, toilet paper was an issue. Stores had empty shelves. Schools would have a lot of the toilet paper that would have been used by the students who were now home. Of course, some of us talked about the olden days of the out houses and the Sears catalogues! I could even talk about the old outhouse from when I was a child. It brought to my mind the memory of me knocking on the door of the outhouse when my grandma's maid was in it and then sneaking to the back and the other side of it when she came out (of course, me, giggling silently). She wanted to know who was doing all that banging on the door. A kind person does not worry about what others may be thinking of them, but that person has a focus that is concentrated on kindness. This could be as little as giving up their seat on a bus or any place because they were listening to the desire of another person. Kindness is being one who is open to share in the good day of another person.

Goodness

Goodness is being virtuous or doing the "right thing" and having others do this as well. The police officers are the ones who enforce the laws so we all can have a peaceful and safe world to live in. Lawyers are also people who help people live their lives justly. Laws for the good of people in the community and country are a necessity for humankind. Bankers and/or loan specialists are people who are filled with goodness of doing what is right. Their every number on paper needs to be done with care and accuracy. This is goodness and a virtuous piece of work.

Long-Suffering

Long-suffering is having or showing patience in spite of troubles, especially those caused by other people or natural disasters. These are the farmers and the people who maintain our roads. Farmers often have to bear the hardships of weather-related crop failures like frost, hail, wind, heavy rains, or drought. They often have to bear the hardships that come with livestock like diseases and sickness. Financially, they bear the challenges of the market prices for their products. People who maintain and create new roads deal with a lot of related disasters, including floods, blizzards, and heavy snowstorms. They also deal with people who disregard their safety and their road signs when they are at work.

Mildness (Gentleness)

Gentleness is having a mild manner. People who are in sales portray this because they have to be a person who is relatable in presenting things and in listening to the other person's needs. Their communication skills have to be of a high level, especially their listening skills. People who work in financial operations are people who have this gentleness as they deal with people's money. Money is the survival thing of all people. The loan officer needs to have that gentleness in working through these big financial decisions in people's lives. They can't just be a person who hears, but they also need to respond to what the other one is saying and expressing.

Faith

Faith is having strong beliefs. Speakers are people of faith because they present with confidence what they strongly believe in their hearts. The best speakers that I have heard are those who had one day been shy. Because of the intensity of their beliefs in their whole heart and mind, they work through the uncomfortableness of that and go for the stronger purpose of trying to make a difference by sharing their beliefs. How is my knowledge of my faith? Do I read the Bible? How long does it take to read the gospel of Mark? Do I know the four main topics of the catechism of my church?

Modesty

Modesty can be when you share a gift you have, like playing a musical instrument and just tell people you enjoy doing it. Modesty can also be when you choose to dress appropriately. This is not just women, but it also pertains to men. Husbands and wives and friends are to keep this in perspective. The question is, how would God want me to dress? What does a true professional working for God look like?

Continency (Self-Control)

Continency means having self-discipline and self-control. Autism caregivers and mental health providers have very intense and important work when it comes to teaching and working with people who have no self-discipline and no self-control. Do we have an attitude of gratitude with those who work in these special fields of work? I know that these are occupations that I would not be good at, so I am grateful for those who are. What needs to be done for these people who haven't learned or been able to have self-discipline in their everyday lives?

Chastity

Chasity means abstaining from intimate relations that are not right. Wrong examples of this are those who promote and support intimate relations in their everyday conversations and their actions by supporting those kinds of movies, magazines, and gatherings that are not appropriate. This is even in just the ordinary language of some people that seems to be accepted as okay or humorous. We need to be people who respect the private space of an individual, which is eighteen inches. People doing the right thing in this area need to be married people, teenagers, priests, religious and single people. All adults need to live a chaste or celibate lifestyle at times. We are respectful humans, not animals. A person who chooses a celibate life can be very in tune and connected to God's gift of creation. A lot of these people have peace and joy that radiates an awesome goodness! Their life is one of excitement and enthusiasm! Do parents make every effort for appropriate respect for life in their talking in their homes? As a child, I was taught that appropriate language was Mr. Cow (not bulls), and there was also the Mrs. Cow!

The Ten Commandments are Laws of Love

The Father of the ideal man, Jesus Christ, is God. Because of His great love for creation, God gave His creation the Ten Commandments. These are ways to love Him and His people so our lives can be filled with joy and peace. Wow! What kind of awesome love is that?

These Ten Commandments *(Laws of Love)* are not some empty or harsh laws. These are loving and helpful ways to live our life by.

Why would we want to ever come close to being intimate or be obedient to a false god? A false god could be several things, like who we spend the most time with or what thing is most dear to us. Being in conversation with God several moments of the day pretty well tells us who our true God is to us. Doing the good that reflects God's love for us several moments of the day pretty well tells us who our true God is to us. False gods could be alcohol, cars, cats, cell phones, computers, dogs, drugs, exercising, food, iPads, Internet, machines, money, movies, sex, sports, television, tools, work, etc.

Communication with our one true God is so essential. The ideal married man prays with his family regularly and prays with his children individually every day (for five to ten minutes). The ideal single man prays with others regularly. The ideal priest or minister visits and prays regularly with new people. The ideal single man does the same. What does praying mean? *Communicating with God* is what praying means. Praying is like air. It's needed to stay alive.

Sometimes our human side unknowingly is so present that are formal prayers can become like a robot. This is reciting prayers without our hearts and minds engaged in the process. Without knowing this and acknowledging our weaknesses in this, we can be modeling a prayer similar to a hypocrite. This may be seen as saying one thing and almost within five minutes doing the opposite of what we just said.

Sometimes I have found myself thinking that I just operated like a robot after Mass, praying the rosary, praying the Stations of the Cross, praying the Liturgy of the Hours, or praying the "Chaplet of Divine Mercy." I know this is not the communicator that I want to be or God wants me to be. Do we remember to pray to be stars for others? Do we pray not to be boring and dull for others? Do I pray to be a saint (hero) in the making? (1)

Why would we want to ever say words that are disrespectful to God? Why would we want to act like a bully? The language of a bully inspires suicides and murders. Why would we use a word that makes fun of God's creation of humans? Making fun of God's creation by using inappropriate words can be so anti-life and disrespectful of God's creation, especially the four-letter word that begins with sixth letter of the alphabet. Let's do everything we can to live with gratitude in our hearts for God's creation of people. Why does society seem to accept this kind of language from men as being somewhat okay? God and His words are so incredibly awesome. Why would we say or do anything that seems like we are slapping God in the face? The ideal priest and single man continually encourage and expect loving language wherever they are. This does not have exceptions for things like "boys will be boys," meaning, that there are different ethic levels for boys and girls.

As a youth, I can remember reciting several words that later I soon began to weep over because of what I had said about the God who has loved me to the point of dying for me. I felt like I had slapped God in the face several times. I hit my finger with a hammer as I was helping build a new hay rack when these words came out of my mouth. (2)

Why would we want to ever miss at least the opportunity of once a week to gather with God's people and listen and contemplate on God's word? Why would we ever want to miss that intimate encounter with Jesus in Holy Communion when we are so awesomely *united with the One* who can make a difference in our life? God is so awesome well beyond the ideal priest that our belief and love of worship stays strong always. This means that ministers and priests are not perfect and our relationship with God needs to be strong or become stronger when theirs is not what it should be. Do I come to Mass out of obligation or because I know and believe that this is a part of God's plan for me to come at least once a week to His house and hear His word and be united with Him in Holy Communion to help me transform my life and live as I need to?

As a teenager with my own car, I remember driving around a few blocks around the church talking to God about rather I needed to make this Sunday churchgoing thing a part of my life. For weeks, I continued my independent research on *why* people did this and if I wanted to do it. I have never missed Mass (except sickness) because I knew it was better for me to go than not to go. So many blessings I have received from this, and I am so grateful to God and the people in my life who helped foster this! I have experienced so many people at church who are bright lights for others! (3)

The ideal man or ideal woman can look at all or most of these and truly recall the action of doing these, then the moment of transforming (changing) this sin or imperfection. Some will have been so sorry that they wept enough to never want to not follow these loving and helpful ways (the Ten Commandments) we were given to live by. This is true contrition and transformation.

The first three laws of love are about our relationship with God.
The next seven laws of love are about our relationship with others.

The ideal man has a vison of what it means to honor a person in an authority position and lives by it. For a married man, honoring the woman in his life who accepts the plan of creation God has for his family is essential, respecting the things she has, the goals she has, the dreams she has and never expecting her to drop them for a last-minute decision of his. Communicating needs and hopes and dreams in an honorable way is what it is to honor the most important, as well as having an obedient and respectful mindset. This respect needs to be an example to their children and taught to them so they know how to honor life. Single men who have a respect for women are promoting life in a very unique and special way.

Honoring a parent and honoring a teacher needs to go hand in hand. Teaching the value of discipline is so important in this world in order to have people with a clear vision of right and wrong and, thus, be able to live it in a solid and healthy way. Like in scripture, we need our "yes" to be "yes" and our "no" to be "no." This is in our homes and in our schools. Consequences, not punishments, need to become a higher priority in homes and schools. If a child has the ability to do homework and does not do it, if a child interrupts learning time, there needs to be a consequence, like detention, no recess, writing explanations about it and then a plan on how this will not happen again. The consequences are to be done with a high explanation of why and not always at the time of the consequence but in the planning time. Some students need the planning to begin before the consequence. We need to never teach that doing wrong is okay by not having a consequence or a make-up for the wrong done. There needs to be an act that says this was not okay and not just a talk with a plan. Without consequences for these actions or an act of making up, we steal from the learning of other students on a continuous time line. In homes, we steal from other family members of the unity and respect all deserve. Being clear on what is right and wrong or what is good and bad is what builds good character and the foundation for a virtuous life.

Honoring those in authority, the people with good character and virtues, are those striving to be the ideal man or ideal woman. (4)

The ideal man would never expect a woman to work a job (if she does it is just an unexpected jackpot or bonus, which is not needed, but it is of her choosing) because her number one job is *life*. She needs to take care of her life and the life of her children, born and unborn. She has the gift and responsibility of participating in and fostering God's creation. Never should she feel like the "modern-day slave" by having an overwhelming amount of responsibilities that comes through too many jobs. How many hours do men spend at jobs? How many hours do women spend at jobs? Why do people so easily accept that forty hours of work is so acceptable for men? Most farmers never work a forty-hour week, and years past, all men worked more than forty hours. Why has this changed? Is it good for families and the world that this has changed? For example, if a woman works at a job all day and then comes home to her husband who has not worked all day, it would appear to be rude and laziness on the part of the man if he is not at least helping with the job of the home. The ideal dad pays child support from conception forward if he is not married. The ideal grandpa pays child support when his son does not. This is just the minimal of survival and respect for life. Motherhood begins at conception. Why doesn't fatherhood? The ideal man needs not to have complete intimacy with a woman unless he is always open to life and ready and willing to be a responsible and a loving dad of a child within the marriage vocation until death. So what kind of drop-in abortions would there be if a man were a man? Would there be a lot less unwanted or unprepared pregnancies? How can a world continue to accept *creation abuse*? Why do abortion clinics exist? Why aren't they being replaced as "daddy's orphan (abandoned baby) homes"? Why are we hiding the truths about the good for others? Creation abuse is so accepted. Just watch the news, watch TV shows, and watch the people around you on their speech and their actions. Does it speak a love for life by all from the moment of conception? What actions are accepted that prevent the respect and acceptance of openness to live as a gift of God's creation?

Family life has nothing to do with "creation abusers" or "bed hoppers." We are not frog families or rabbit families. Single people are to be humans living this openness to life as well. The ideal married man loves the life of his children so much that he doesn't let a day pass without giving them a blessing and some words that uplift and of gratitude. This is a true believer in the gift of God's creation! So many people of today say they are pro-life, but it seems so false for the most part. I don't think they realize what they are saying. Saying something without actions is primarily what I see. From my perspective, a woman can only say she is pro-life if she has carried and nourished a baby for nine months and then gives birth. Then she *is* pro-life. By her words and her actions, she states that she is pro-life. Men begin life and can fully support life by their words and supportive actions. What are ten supportive actions men can have to support life? What are ten habits of supporting living a holy life?

I am forever grateful for the life of each of my children, grandchildren, and great-grandchildren! Participating in God's creation is a unique gift beyond human understanding! (5)

The ideal married man has a lot of regular events in his relationship with his wife: the sharing of meals as much as possible, a massage for his wife (a massage man equals a wonderful wife), always doing the garbage, always having a morning act of appreciation (like the coffee on). It may vary, but these are things that are important and meaningful to their spouse. Doing things for his wife is a significant evidence of his commitment to the relationship and family life. *Love without action is dead.* Friendship, in its fullness, enhances the family environment. The ideal man never asks a woman to use contraceptives because of his love for life in its fullness. This goes with the mentality of creation abuse, which is good for no man or woman. God created a woman as she is, and no man should even consider micromanaging it with pills, condoms, pressures, briberies, etc. The highest respect and dignity and gratitude are what are needed in men's hearts toward women each day. God chose woman to be intimately involved in His plan for creation. God chose man to begin each moment of this creation. What a gift and a miracle this truly is! (6)

The ideal man knows what it means to physically steal from others and what it means to spiritually steal from others. When a man so "micromanages" the members of the family so they do not take the time to be intimate with the most important One (God) in their life, this is stealing spiritually of each member and the family as a whole. Time spent spiritually nourishing each member of the family by regularly and creatively praying with them is the man's role as the father in the home. The question each day needs to be, "Am I stealing any time or fruitfulness from my family today?" Always remember not to follow the example of the chipmunks who steal their food (nuts) from one another just because they have the ability to store about six thousand per year! (7)

What man would choose to lie? *Honesty* even if it hurts, is so life-giving! Lying and not being accountable is pretty much the same vein. Saying that you are going to do something and failing to do it, except for emergencies, is not being honest and trustworthy.

Saying that we love life and then give attention to what color of skin people have is talking falsely. Information forms that ask for people's culture lack a respect for life. Some of us have a half of a dozen cultures in our background. Why does that matter? Why do we avoid sticking to the real issues of doing right without excuses of culture or background? The truth is we are all people made in God's image. For example, is a yellow crayon any better than a brown crayon? Is a blue crayon any better than a red crayon? Is a white crayon any better than a black crayon? No, they are all crayons with different looks and potential when they are used independently or together. Why do we have this mess when it comes to the color of people's skin? Why do we have this mess when it comes to different cultures? All people have different potentials and different gifts, but we are all people. There is a difference of good and bad actions of individual people. This is false speech when it is mixed into skin color groups or culture groups.

What kind of truth do we speak through our words and actions each day about the children or people of God? My dad taught me that dishonesty was at the top of the worst things to do. A comment that I think this is needed in today's world on this same vein of honesty is "You won't need to be sorry now if you hadn't done what you did. Do things right the first time and always and you won't have a need to be sorry." (8)

What married man would look at another woman or take delight in who she is? This is not only the neighbor or the waitress or coworker or friend, etc. The only "deer" in his mind needs to be focused on is his spouse. This is the one to admire, chase, and take delight in. For farmers, the "John Deere" needs to be second! How grateful are we for the married women and men in this world? (9)

Why be interested in the neighbors "M&M's" (Mercedes and Mustang)? Obsessing and drooling over the neighbors' goods does not inspire for one's own good family life. So why take the time to be jealous of it? How grateful are we for the things we have in this world? (10)

The ideal men would plan more gatherings of "prayer," while the ideal women would plan more gatherings of "parties." She would plan family parties celebrating with gratitude, birthdays and baptisms, being so thankful for physical life and spiritual life within for each member of their family!

The Ten Commandments

In the Old Testament

Exodus 20:1-17   Deuteronomy 5:7-21

1. I Am the Lord your God. You shall not have strange gods before Me.
2. You shall not use the name of the Lord your God in vain.
3. Remember to keep holy the Lord's Day.
4. Honor your father and your mother.
5. You shall not kill.
6. You shall not commit adultery.
7. You shall not steal.
8. You shall not lie or bear false witness against your neighbor.
9. You shall not covet your neighbor's wife.
10. You shall not covet your neighbor's goods.

Are we allowing our world to turn into a world of human pigs, sows and boars? Have we turned off our brains and quit doing self-talk to do what is right for family life and are now choosing living more like the animals focused on "my" pleasure? These ten laws of love are to help us live a full and complete life.

The New Testament Writers

8

Tradition states that there are primarily eight writers, teachers, and preachers in the New Testament.

Matthew

Matthew gave facts as he lived his life and often in the presence of Jesus Christ. He was on the mission to have people come to know Jesus not only through his writings, but also as he taught and preached. His writings were primarily written in the 70s. His beliefs in Jesus were presented to so many people. Do we spend time writing our thoughts and ideas about Jesus in our life? Do we write our plans about what we believe? Do we write our thoughts on what we believe God wants us to do today? Do we write our thought and ideas on how we think we have responded to what we think God has asked us to do? A tax collector did this. Would we be a better person if we spent five or ten minutes each day writing and focusing?

Mark

Mark wrote the shortest gospel. He speaks of Jesus being a servant and one who made great sacrifices. He wrote his gospel primarily in the year 60. He wrote about the overwhelming number of miracles that he experienced. Do we write and share with others all the miracles that we experience in our lives? Do we even pay enough attention to see them and recognize them?

Luke

Luke wrote a lot about our salvation history. He writes about events of Jesus and the church. His writings were most probably written between 80 and 90. Do we write about salvation history? Do we teach or even share in our daily conversations events in salvation history? How knowledgeable and in touch are we with our salvation history? If the big Bible seems overwhelming or too much, try reading a children's Bible or a teen's Bible. Just doing it for a different perspective can also broaden one's way of seeing the messages God has for us!

John

John was known as the divine because of his theological brilliance. He wrote about women in the gospel with respect and without seeing them as inferior but seeing them as an asset to the community. He shares a lot about the wondrous deeds of Jesus. This gospel was written between 90 and 100. He was known as the beloved disciple and spoke a lot about the "signs" of love Jesus did for others. Do we share the signs of love we see our family members give? Do we show gratitude for all the love we experience through others, or do we take it for granted? Do we share on how we see others in how they are so bad at giving love and seek ways to resolve this sad story?

Peter

Peter wrote or inspired someone to write
1 Peter and 2 Peter letters in the New Testament. He is mentioned more in the gospels than any other disciple. He teaches and preaches that Christianity is the true religion, even in the midst of great persecutions. He calls himself a servant of Jesus and teaches a lot about living a life with Christian virtue. Do we value our gift of Christianity? Do we value having been taught the goodness of living a life by virtues?

James

James's letter was written about 90-100. He speaks of trials and tribulations and the good that can come from them. Just pause for a few minutes and reflect on any trials and tribulations that come to mind. Did any good come from them? Do we share these things with others to help uplift them when they are going through tough times? People are encouraged to be doers of the word and to be people of prayer. Do we pray with our heart and with our actions? Do we listen to the word and respond with loving actions?

Jude

Jude's letter was to the heretics, those who opposed the law and authority. They were denying that Jesus is Lord. It was written between 62 and 67. Do we hear and listen to any warnings that Jesus speaks of in His word? Do we search for these messages in the word so we can know them and live by them?

Paul

Paul, one of the most creative writers, wrote several letters in the New Testament. He had a lot of things to share, all from his mission work to several areas. He faced a lot of resistance in his teachings of Jesus as our Lord and Savior. He even spent time in prison where he continued his writings. How much writing do I do? Do I know what value daily journaling could be? Have I done any research on this so I could have a better opportunity to become a believer in it?

The Beatitudes

8

These Beatitudes are from Matthew 5:1-12.

They are also known as blessings.

*1. **Blessed are the poor in spirit, for theirs is the kingdom of heaven.***

Being poor in spirit means that we are to be dependent on God and we are not to be dependent on the things of this world. We are not to have a love of riches or money. We are to prioritize our choices. We are to be grateful for the gift of the time given to each of us. I know that I could do much better at this. If I was more dependent on God, I would be a more generous person.

*2. **Blessed are the meek, for they shall possess the land.***

Being meek is standing by God's truth and not backing down. We are not to be timid or a person of temper when it comes to doing and supporting what is right in God's eyes. I would be better at standing by God's truth if I spent more time in prayer, communicating with God.

*3. **Blessed are they who mourn, for they shall be comforted.***

Being a person of mourning is one who is sad for one's sins and asks for forgiveness. They will be comforted by the Holy Spirit. Those who hide their sin or try to justify their sins will not be comforted. If we would be acting differently, if God was in the room or wherever we are, we probably have some things in our world that need to change. I have often seen people mourn as they go to the sacrament of reconciliation. This is inspiring to me to see someone truly repenting of their sins.

These first three Beatitudes are faults that need to be corrected in order to enter the kingdom of God (heaven). We are to be dependent on God. We are to always stand by the truth. We are to always desire Jesus. We are to be truly sorry for our sins.

4. **Blessed are they who hunger and thirst after justice, for they shall have their fill.**

Those who deeply desire justice in this world and live their desire by the many things they do will have peace and joy. When laws are not just, when people do not treat others in a just way in their social environments, and when family members make statements that do not display justice, do we stand up for the truth in our words and our actions?

5. **Blessed are the merciful, for they shall obtain mercy.**

Those who are truly sorry for what they have done wrong and dedicate the rest of their life never to do it again and give totally to make up for that wrong are those who will have peace and joy. Do you know the "Chaplet of Divine Mercy Prayer"? It is a prayer that gives one a sense of peace. In scripture, it states the number of times one is to forgive is not seven times, but seven times seventy!

6. **Blessed are the clean of heart, for they shall see God.**

Those who give seek God wholeheartedly and are not just a lukewarm Christian will have peace and joy.

These previous three beatitudes focus on the virtues of justice, mercy, and purity. They are essential for a good relationship with God and our neighbors.

7. **Blessed are the peacemakers, for they shall be called the children of God.**

Being a follower of Jesus requires teaching and preaching the message of peace by daily words and examples. In doing this, we will be called the children of God because we will be acting like we are.

8. **Blessed are they who suffer persecution for justice's sake, for theirs is the kingdom of heaven.**

Being a follower of Jesus and sharing His messages requires sacrifices and sufferings. At times one will feel persecuted, but one does it anyway because the kingdom of heaven is then theirs.

These last two beatitudes urge Christ's followers to spread peace and the gospel message.

Intermission Time!

The ideal man does not think he knows more than a woman on cars, directions, everything, money, sports, tech, tools, or women! Right?

The Capital Sins

7

The ideal man can tell you what the seven capital (worst) sins are because he lives a life striving to *not* do them.

Anger

Anger in the source from which injuries of another flow.

To help us avoid this sin, practice calmness and
peace and the heavenly virtue of patience.

Matthew 5:22

**"But I say to you, whoever is angry to his
brother will be liable to judgment."**

Envy

Envy is ingratitude and belittling another.
To help us avoid this sin, practice prayer, praying for the best
interests of others, and the heavenly virtue of kindness.

Acts of the Apostles 7:9

**"And patriarchs, jealous of Joseph, sold him into
slavery in Egypt; but God was with him."**

Gluttony

Gluttony is an unregulated love for food or drink.
To help us avoid this sin, practice fasting and self-
denial and the heavenly virtue of abstinence.

1 Corinthians 10:31

**"So whether you eat or drink, or whatever you
do, do everything for the glory of God."**

Greed

Greed is love of worldly goods.
To help us avoid this sin, practice generosity and
kindness and the heavenly virtue of charity.
1 Timothy 6:10
**"For the love of money is the root of all evils and some
people in their desire for it have strayed from the faith
and have pierced themselves with many pains."**

Lust

Lust is desiring an inappropriate intimacy with another person.
To help us avoid this sin, practice thankfulness and
sacrificing and the heavenly virtue of chastity.
Colossians 3:5
**"Put to death, then, the parts of you that are earthly: immorality,
impurity, passion, evil desire, and the greed that is idolatry."**

Pride

Pride is self-love and the opposite of living for God.
To help us avoid this sin, practice self-denial and
the heavenly virtue of humility.
Proverbs 16:18
"Pride goes before disaster, and a haughty spirit before a fall."

Sloth

Sloth is a laziness of mind and body and spiritual growth.
To help us avoid this sin, practice prayer, the sacraments and
spiritual readings, and the heavenly virtue of diligence.
Exodus 5:8
**"Yet you shall levy upon them the same quota of
bricks as they have previously made. Do not reduce it.
They are lazy; that is why they are crying."**

The Deacons

7

Acts of the Apostles 6:5

Deacons are for building the church.

They are men ordained to serve the community as leaders of prayer, liturgical *celebrations, teaching and preaching.*

A transitional deacon is a man who plans to become a priest and is only a deacon temporarily. It is known as the final preparation stage before priesthood.

A permanent deacon is a man who makes a lifelong commitment to serve either as a celibate or in the married diaconate.

As part of the preparation, they become a lector, an acolyte, and make a public commitment to celibacy. If he is married, this is to be his only wife. Both deacons complete the required study for their position. They are to forever pray the Liturgy of the Hours, the prayer of the church.

Their ministry may include assisting with Christian initiation, the ministry of the word, assisting the priest during the liturgy of the Eucharist. It also can include leading benediction, leading the rite of marriage from the Roman ritual, leading in intercessions before communal reconciliation services, leading Liturgy of the Hours in the parish community, minister of communion to the sick, and leader of Christian burial services. Other services are preparing families for the baptism of their infant and leading the celebration of the baptism. They can also bless objects and people within certain liturgical celebrations.

The First Seven Deacons

Timon was said to have been a Hellenized Jew who became a bishop in Syria. He ministered to widows and was thrown into a furnace as his martyrdom. He is a saint of the church.

Philip preached the gospel in Samaria and had many converts. He was also known as an evangelist. He is a saint of the church.

Stephen was a great preacher and a persuasive and brave deacon in the early church at Jerusalem. He served and taught the poor. He is known as the first Christian who was martyred for this faith by being stoned to death. He is a saint of the church.

Nicanor ministered to the requiring needs in the holy city of Jerusalem. According to tradition, he was martyred at Cyprus and is a saint of the church.

Nicholas was a proselyte from Antioch. He converted to Judaism, a miracle worker, and a martyr.

Parmenas was said to have preached in Asia Minor. He was martyred for his faith at Philippi according to tradition. He is a saint of the church.

Prochorus, tradition states, helped take care of the poor in Jerusalem, and his life was ended in Antioch as he became a martyr. He is a saint of the church.

1 Timothy 3:8-12

There are nine qualifications for deacons according to the New Testament letter. Simply stated, these are: respected by others, shows credibility in their beliefs, not addicted to drinking, a non-lover of money, behaves consistently with their beliefs, gives service to the church, has a wife respected by others, a "one-woman man," and a spiritual leader of his wife and children.

How much do we know about deacons in our church? Do we see a need for more deacons? Would this help our church and world? Check with God to see if you might be missing your call. Check with God to see if you might be missing seeing the gifts of a man and/or couple who might be missing the call because no one brought it to their attention. Would this help others become an ideal man and/or ideal woman?

The Gifts of the Holy Spirit

7

Isaiah 11:2

Awe (Fear of the Lord)

**To give glory and praise to God and to acknowledge
*that all created things are gifts from God.***

This is what we do when we go to Mass during the week or on the weekend. Doesn't it seem a little bit like walking into heaven? The artwork is so beautiful with so many memories of Jesus and His miracles of love. The altar is so beautiful! The candles burning and the quiet peaceful atmosphere is such a calming and stress-free experience! People are talking to God and listening to God in so many different ways. Some people are just silently sitting and enjoying God's presence and feeling like they are in God's home. They are at peace and so grateful for no job demands, no fighting, no noise, no hostility, and no negativity. Others are begging for God's help. Either way, it can become a very hopeful moment in time. Sometimes we just don't understand how broken we are. Sometimes we don't realize how great the saving power of God is. This fear of the Lord can be the beginning of wisdom. What kind of fears have we experienced in our lives? Were we totally connected to God at these times, or were we innocently just experiencing the reality of human events? In my childhood, some moments of fear were grabbing the eggs under a hen, learning how to ride a bike, hearing someone breaking into our home, and sneaking around the big tree to give my grandma's maid a push on the hammock (knowing that I could be in trouble). In my youth, some moments of fear were falling off the hay rack, getting a speeding ticket, and getting home too late. What moments of fear do we experience? Do we share our fears with God and others so we can develop a stronger awe *for our God rather than a fear? Do we realize that every action we make is not hidden from God? So if our actions are having nothing to fear, we must be very much engaged on what God wants for our life! When we keep the focus on heaven, we are in* awe *with our God!*

Counsel

To make right judgments through reflection, prayer, and action and to help others do the same.

Making right judgments begins with our value of life. We will have a pro-life world when the ideal man who supports life says, "I am only a strong supporter of the life of the unborn. It is that woman who carries and nourishes that baby for nine months and who gives birth who is truly and honestly the pro-life person." In making judgments, can a man be man enough to tell a woman that he is not ready or not prepared to be a daddy, or can a woman be grateful enough of the "gift of being the one to participate in God's gift of creation" to tell a man that she is not ready or not prepared to be a mommy by living the "no" or "no, not now" words? Are they experiencing an empty love tank at too early of age? Are too many people aching inside to make right judgments? Can we get more order in our daily lives by sticking with the truth? Boring is okay sometimes. Can we have more holy things in our homes? What creative actions can each of us take to better live in right judgment?

Fortitude

To give courageous witness to our faith and to issues of peace and justice for all.

The men who give courageous witness to faith and justice for all are those who stand in and support the baby/child who is abandoned by their daddy or mommy. I have seen grandpas and grandmas raise the grandchildren. There are a lot of independent actions that can be done to give hope for these abandoned ones. Any child who lacks in physical, emotional, intellectual, and spiritual needs is experiencing abandonment. What does it take to change this? Do we want to advance in our faith? Take time in silence and listen to what moves your heart from God's word. By doing this, we can be moved to being a "sign" of God's love in the world. Are we striving to be a prayer book of faith? What weeds do we need to get rid of?

Knowledge

To learn God's plan for us by using our gifts of spiritual insight.

Is the only place a child grows in knowledge is at school with people who are not of the family? Do schools unite enough with parents and parents unite with schools enough to make this process of growing in knowledge effective and efficient? Do schools give families enough time and resources/support to take care of the physical, emotional, and spiritual needs of their children? Personally, sometimes I can get very frustrated with the educated and think and wonder how certain decisions that are made seem dumber than a box of rocks. Some schools can spend so much time for sports and practices that it cuts out time for spiritual knowledge and nourishment. Schools sometimes spend so much time on disciplining a few students while the rest of the students are cheated of a good education. Schools sometimes have way too much time spent on fun and parties that good learning time is taken away. Sometimes schools have such low expectations, like having no homework, that some students get bored and choose things that are not good. Some schools are doing excellent, but none are perfect, so all could kick things up a notch for the good of the students and the parents. Those schools (teachers) that are doing an excellent job need a higher respect and more pay. I have seen some teachers spending time working double shifts like Monday through Friday, from 7:00 a.m. to 10:00 p.m., and also Saturdays for the good of their students. Some teachers have very needy students and go the extra miles to help them. What are we doing to make better the lives of these people who are doing so much? What are we doing with those who need to do better? Do we ignore them? How many families have the discipline of reading in their homes?

Piety (Love)

To recognize God as giver of all good gifts and to treat others and all creation with reverence.

The people who are givers of good gifts and treat others and all creation with reverence are people who work at a birthright office. Doctors and nurses are also those who treat others with reverence. They are there for promoting the good health and life of another. Spiritual leaders who spend a lot of their time communicating and encouraging others truly recognize God as the giver of all good gifts. Is there anything that we need to do after reflecting on this?

Understanding

To keep open minds as we search for faith and truth wherever it leads.

It takes learning and listening to become a person with understanding and empathy. The one who is practicing this on a daily basis is making a decision to love and making the decision to connect and relate. How well do we live the "decision to love"? Is love a feeling to just enjoy only?

Wisdom

The ability to recognize our limitations and strengths and to deepen our experience of God.

Do we have a deep wisdom when it comes to the gift of life? How grateful are we of the gift of life to have the privilege and responsibility to participate in the moment of its beginning? How grateful are we of the gift of life to be the essential nourishers of that life for the first nine months? Men can only say they are against abortion. Women can say they are for abortion but give life to a baby. What is our perspective on the essential truths about life?

The Last Words of Christ

7

Father, forgive them,
For they do not know what they are doing.
—Luke 23:34

Woman, here is your son . . .
Here is your mother . . .
—John 19:26-27

I Am thirsty.
—John 19:28

Truly I tell you, today you will be with Me in paradise.
—Luke 23:43

My God, my God, why have You forsaken Me?
—Mark 15:34

It is finished.
—John 19:30

Father, into Your hands, I command My Spirit.
—Luke 23:46

These last words of Jesus are filled with so much love for me and all of us!
How I need to spend more time uniting myself to His words. This sacrificing
was for our sins. Sin is heartbreaking and a tragedy. We need to forgive but not

forget because we need to protect ourselves and others from evil or harm, but forgiveness is bearing another person's burden and going the extra mile. Strive to admire and find the good and quit wasting time with comparing people. Only the true love comes from God.

The Moral Virtues

7

Patriotism

Patriotism is having tremendous support for one's country. Many people join the armed forces to help protect the lives and rights of the people of their country. A story of patriotism is one of my family members who fought in World War 2 and forever carried that mark on his chin that was injured from bullet fragments. Another story is another family member of my husband who was the only one remaining alive on the front lines of the battlefield and how he was lost for a time. Another story is of an in-law's family member who had the job of picking up the dead bodies on the battlefield. What acts of gratitude do we personally make because of others who made the sacrifices for all of us to have life and/or a better life?

Obedience

Obedience is behavior that is respectful and mindful of rules and laws. A story of obedience is parents who teach their children good manners and respect, especially for others and the elderly. When these children visit their grandparents, they are more like angel children. What a joy this is to experience! These same children are most probably the angel children in the classroom and on the playground. What a joy this is to experience! People who understand the reasons of God's laws of love and are obedient to them give much hope to the world! Another story of obedience is when the medical professionals give advice for the good of all, and others respond in concern and willingness to do their part for the sake of the health of others. This also gives hope to the world! What do we do in respect and response to those who promote the goodness of life for all of us?

Veracity

Veracity is honesty. A story of veracity is from my childhood. This was the one of the worst things one could do is be dishonest. If one wanted to have a good life, the number one thing was to be honest. This does not include little fibs, little white lies, and barely even making a little honest mistake. Little dishonest things were equal to big dishonesty because that is where it would lead to. Over sixty years ago, I can remember it as good as if it happened yesterday, my dad making a great emphasis on honesty and its value. He was sitting by the stove after we had our family evening meal, making this point of life very clear. I have great difficulty when any adult requires a child to say "I am sorry." Oftentimes, in my mind, this is teaching dishonesty. If a child is in tears and shows signs of being sorry, and an adult could ask them if they are sorry, and if they would like to choose to go tell them that then, this seems to be an honest act coming from the heart. When an adult makes a child say "I am sorry" to another when there is a chance the child is not sorry, they are teaching them to lie. When a child or youth receives no consequences from their bad or wrong actions, this is also teaching dishonesty. Right and wrong are so important to the lives of all people. Being dishonest on paying taxes or any money transactions and being dishonest in a relationship are areas where a lot of hurt and pain can come in one's life and spread to other lives. What areas of dishonesty do we need to take a look and change? Most everyone probably has some little areas of dishonesty that need to be cleaned up.

Liberality

Liberality is making expenditures for the benefit of others, not being stingy. A story of liberality is having parties that recognize the value of another like birthday parties, anniversary parties, graduation parties, etc. A lot of parents help their children with college or car expenses. This can be a good thing to do. Sometimes children help their parents with their expenditures. This can be a good thing too. A lot of children are taught to be generous and to share with others. These children are already practicing living with a caring heart. What areas of our life can we do something to be more generous and less stingy?

Patience

Patience is to suffer for a purpose without getting upset. This is controlling one's emotions, and this is often called a saint activity. Patient people have a respect for time and practice slowing down and thinking before speaking. A patient person makes great efforts to deal with the discomfort that is presented in their day to day activities. They take the time before doing things, especially in times of discomfort. A story of patience is the parents of a strong-willed child. What areas of our lives do we practice patience? What areas of our lives do we need to practice more patience?

Humility

Humility is taking care of others. The opposite of humility is pride. Pride is one doing everyday things for oneself. It is a person making efforts to grasp divinity for oneself. Humility is about kindness, patience, and charity to others. This is submitting to the Lord in all we do and in every part of our lives. A humble person recognizes the parts of their life that need some work. A humble person has empathy for others and takes responsibility to not hurt others physically or mentally by their actions. A humble person learns to love the simple things. They purposely take the lower position. They give without wanting to impress another. A story of humility is the life of Mother Theresa. How do we practice humility in our lives? What can we do to be more of a humble person?

Purity

Purity is freedom from immorality, freedom from guilt or evil, and freedom from vices or negativity. A story of purity is Mary, the mother of Jesus, the woman who lived her life without sin or evil. Other stories of purity are some of the saints and heroes of this world who only do good for another. The ideal man is one who is a daddy from the beginning to the end. This is a person who is a true lover of life. What areas do we practice purity in our lives?

These moral virtues are so good for all of us to deepen our knowledge of what truly is good. I especially hope that all politicians would seriously spend more time on these simple virtues. The politicians have the authority and responsibility to make good decisions for all people of the country. Let us pray that all of us make a deeper connection and have a deeper relationship with God.

The Sacraments

7

Sacraments are visible signs that give grace.

They are gifts that are given!

(These sacraments are known as sacraments of initiation)

Baptism (Galatians 3:27)

Baptism is an encounter with Jesus when we become a member of the spiritual family, the church. We become a child of God. Our original sin and all sins are washed away, and we become clean to continue to live in the family of the church. The main sign is the pouring of water.

This gift was so awesome when each of my six children became members of God's family, the people of the church, at their baptism! What a blessing to be participating in physical life of God's creation and then participating in the spiritual life of God's creation!

Confirmation (John 15:26)

Confirmation is an encounter with Jesus when we are especially strengthened with the Holy Spirit to guide us in our everyday life on our journey with the Lord. We are now a full soldier in the army against sin in the world. The main sign is the laying on of hands and the anointing of chrism oil.

This gift is usually celebrated in the last few years as a teenager. I believe it needs to be given at an earlier age. People my age celebrated it primarily in third grade. It is not the end of religion education. It is primarily the beginning that needs to last forever in order to be a dedicated soldier in God's army. For me, it was so cool to become a soldier for Christ at this early age! It truly was a "wow" moment in my life! Some children/youth may have a different age level that is more appropriate than others. With consultations with the parents on when this is would be my suggestion because family and church could be more united at this moment on our spiritual journey.

Eucharist (Luke 22:14-20)

The Eucharist is an encounter with Jesus when we are personally and completely united with Him, when we receive the body and blood of Jesus in Holy Communion. At Mass, the bread and wine are changed into the body and blood of Jesus. This takes place daily at the Mass celebrated in churches throughout the world. I will never know enough of God's word. So often I just don't get all the richness and wisdom of the messages in the Bible, so I truly need to hear and study it more. Being united with Jesus in Holy Communion is so wonderful! I need so much help to transform so many things in my life!

The year before I made my first communion, I was selected to be a flower girl, who helped lead all the first communion children into the church! I am so grateful for so many opportunities in my life that I was asked to lead others in church activities and/or events!

(These are known as sacraments of service.)

Matrimony (Mark 10:6-9)

Matrimony is an encounter with Jesus when a man and woman make a forever commitment to each other to love each other and be open to the new lives of children they are blessed with and to give physical, emotional, intellectual, and spiritual nourishment to them and each other. Their sacrificial love is to be in union with the sacrificial love of Jesus Christ. Their rings are to be the sign of this unconditional love. I am not sure of the new-age belief that people need to be a certain age to get married. (I was eighteen, and I have family members who were in their teens and are still married today.) Sometimes a man and a woman in a marriage need to part because of the inability of them to settle their differences or their inability to recognize sin and change their lives. Marriage is a sacrament that goes hand in hand with God and believing always that anything is possible with God. Love is a continuous decision and not just a feeling of pleasure. Happy and joyful moments are times to be grateful. The more unselfish people are, the more these moments of joy seem to just happen.

Holy Orders (1 Peter 2:5)

Holy Orders is an encounter with Jesus when a man makes a forever commitment to Christ and His church (the people) in love and service. Some of them who are close to being ideal men have been helped and mentored by a woman who was close to being an ideal woman! He is to be the spiritual leader who helps the people live their lives in union with the sacrificial love of Jesus Christ. During his ordination, the laying on hands by the bishop and his commitment to preach the word are a part of this life of service.

As a young child, I used to play church on the front porch doing prayers, having dishes from the house, and then making mud pies. Allowing children to imagine and pretend they are adults is something that our young people and our world has/is choosing to miss out on. We all need time to dream and imagine in order for us to have progress in our physical, emotional, intellectual areas of our life. The clergy that have helped me in my journey of many years are not so much the preachers, but the supporters and encouragers and listeners. Examples of good church leaders are those who are prayerful because their prayer then radiates through their every action. This has helped me, and it also continues to help my faith life tremendously!

(These sacraments are known as sacraments of healing.)

Reconciliation (Colossians 1:20)

Reconciliation is an encounter with Jesus when we ask for mercy for our sins and make the firm commitment to sin no more. The priest prays for us to be absolved of our sins by God. God offers His love and mercy. The blessing and handshake of peace are a part of this sacrament. Having been a director of religious education for years, I came to strongly believe in the sacraments as a gift.

One time there was a second-grade student who was unable to attend most of the preparation classes, and I was not sure if he should receive the sacrament or if he should wait. After talking with the dad and listening to him, I agreed to go ahead with the sacrament. A week later, the student died from a sudden illness. I was so grateful and became a strong believer in the sacraments as being gifts from God for our church family. Sometimes, for me, reconciliation is a time of "trition," when I am sorry for my sins. Sometimes, for me, reconciliation is a time of "contrition," when my heart is moved with deep sorrow by weeping.

Reconciliation/confession can be an uncomfortable experience. After all, what woman really wants to go to a man and tell their faults? I have worked long and hard with a lot of self-talk that I am going to God, and this human priest is just the human person who is representing the true God. Rather, he is a partial sinner or a full-time sinner is not my judgment call. I am seeking forgiveness and a new step on my human faith journey to the kingdom. To make this experience more relatable and a little less stressful, I believe having this sacrament celebrated in the environment of God's creation could be a fruitful and good step. The two most recent examples of this have been when college students were asked to take a short ride on a golf cart, go to confession, and then return to the designated spot, and another was people going to confession from their car window in a church parking lot. I believe having these kinds of sacrament opportunities at church festivals and on weekends would be great—"confessions on the go"!

Anointing of the Sick (James 5:14)

Anointing of the sick is an encounter with Jesus when we are provided the grace of the Holy Spirit and encouraged and strengthened when we are experiencing anxiety and evils to bring us to trust in God. It enables us to unite our pains with Christ pains and death. This sacrament prepares us for our entrance into heaven. The practice of celebrating the sacrament of reconciliation often and living the virtues of faith, hope, and love while doing the will of God is all in preparation for heaven. The blessing and prayer of the priest with anointed oils are a part of this sacrament.

As a youth, I remember the priest driving out to our farm to give my dad the sacrament, anointing of the sick (extreme unction). I also remember my dad getting well from his very high fever after that in a short time. This sacrament is so good for the person who is ill as well as the family of the ill person.

These sacraments are celebrations of encountering Christ. Over fifty years ago, when I was a senior in high school, the only homework that I remember having was writing a paper on the seven sacraments, and each explanation of the sacraments was to begin with the name of the sacrament and then the words "is an encounter with Jesus," followed by the meaning and symbol of each sacrament. Because I wrote these sacraments down with an explanation of each, I gained a deeper understanding and commitment to them.

Would this spiritual exercise of writing and reflecting help others in understanding and responding in love to these sacraments? All these sacraments are gifts, so it concerns me greatly when they are denied by church leaders. To me, there is a difference between being denied and being delayed. Of course, I do not know the full stories, and church leaders are human too.

The Unities of the Church

THE SEVEN UNITIES

How are these unities taught and lived by the teachers and preachers of the church?

Ephesians 4:4-6

One Church

What does that mean? One perspective on this would be at the beginning of life. Are we one with the family of God at the very beginning of life? Does the ideal man appreciate the gift of having that gift, the privilege, of being the one to begin life?

Our church family has a way of helping everyone feel one with one another by having colors in the liturgical celebrations that have meaning. This is their symbolic meanings: black is for mourning, green is for hope and for life, pink is for joy in a time of penance, purple is for penance, red is for offering one's life to God, gold is for the highest of celebrations, and white is for integrity and purity of life. These are seven colors. The vestments that are worn are to give meaning to the celebration. The vestments are to help everyone put their focus on the real ideal man, Jesus Christ.

One Spirit

What does that mean? One perspective on this would be at the beginning of life. Are we one with the Spirit at the time of conception? Is this a moment that has been guided with the Holy Spirit? Do we teach this as being the good way of life?

One Faith

What does that mean? Is the beginning of life only a pleasure moment, or is it a faith moment? If it is only a pleasure moment, then this is an abortion mentality and not pro-life mentality. Does everyone spend every day in a pro-life mentality in all aspects of life? If not, then one is living an abortion mentality. How honest are we being in today's world with this? Does pro-life only pertain to the nine months before the event of a "physical birth"? Only a woman can be the one who carries and nourishes the baby for nine months and then give birth. The man was not given this gift. So only a woman can truly and honestly be pro-life in action and word. Only a man can be the daddy who was meant to be, beginning at conception. How does a man live being the daddy? It takes being "one in faith" to be a true family person.

One Hope

What does that mean? At the beginning of life, the daddy and mommy can be "one in hope" by praying and living God's will at this time and forever. The mommy is to nourish the baby physically by eating, exercising, and getting enough sleep, as well as participating in all appointments with the doctor that are recommended. The daddy is to physically support the mommy by paying all the expenses for this so mommy has no stress, which is important for the life of their baby. The daddy and mommy need to emotionally support each other by being loving and kind to each other as well as talking to their baby. They need to study how their baby is developing and study how to be good parents. Educating themselves is only doing the right thing and responsible thing. It is time to begin reading to their baby. Spiritual life for each needs another kick upward to give strength and "right focus" on the decisions to come. Blessing their baby each day and praying together is living in "one faith and one hope with the One Lord." Praying and blessing only takes less than five minutes. We all have time for the most important things in our life. A blessing can be just making a cross on the baby/child. Spiritual and physical nourishment go hand in hand.

One Lord

What does that mean? We are in the world experiencing God's creation that is beyond our human understanding! We are one with the Lord as we live each day of our own creation! How much do we teach and share with others in our knowledge of the gifts of creation? Families that fish together, families that pray together privately and publicly, families that work together, and families that play together are showing gratitude for their experience of being created and participating in His creation. Those who walk in this union with the Lord are striving for holiness and are saints (heroes) in the making. Matthew 5:48, "So be perfect, just as your heavenly Father is perfect." *Some ways to soar spiritually are pay attention to God's way by having scheduled time daily to discern this. (At the end of the day, reflect on where I was blessed and where I was closed.) Keep the commandments because of gratitude for being loved so much and not because of obligation. Strive to be a person of charity.*

One Baptism

What does that mean? When we are baptized in the church family, we become a member. This is only the beginning of the spiritual life that continues until heaven or hell. So nourishment in this spiritual life is important daily and weekly. What choices are there to make this a true practice? Talking to God, listening and living His word, offering our joys and burdens to God, and uniting ourselves with Him while striving to transform the imperfections in our lives with gratitude in our hearts for our blessings are some of the ways we can respond. What kind of models are daddies and mommies giving to their children in whom they were so blessed to be a part of that creation?

One God and Father of All

What does that mean? At the beginning of life, are we fully open to being a daddy? Are we fully open to being a mommy? Are we one with God who is the Father of us all? Do we continue to live this way until death of each of us? That is sacrificing and enjoying one another in living God's will fully alive and one until we join the greatest giver of life!

Are we united in the ways that are shared above? Are we united as being one with unimportant media and not God and family? Are we united as being one in the game of sports and not God and family? Are we united as being one with our pets and not God and family?

The Number 7 in the Bible
has significance or meaning: fullness or completeness.

The Rosary

Why pray the rosary? It has been said that the family who prays together, stays together. A lot of miracles have been connected to the rosary. For me, the rosary gives me peace. If I am experiencing stress, reflecting on these fabulous events in the life of Jesus gives me a renewed focus and purpose. I have made a commitment to never pray the rosary when I am driving by myself because I become so at peace that I often fall asleep while on the road. In knowing this, I make the decision to respect my life and the lives of others by choosing the time and place that is not sinful. One does not have to be a Catholic to pray the rosary. Reflecting and meditating on the events of the life of Jesus is a good practice for anyone who believes in Jesus.

THE GLORIOUS MYSTERIES OF THE ROSARY

5

The First Glorious Mystery: The Resurrection

This is the event when Jesus rose from the dead. We celebrate this event on Easter Sunday! **(Mark 16:6)**

The Second Glorious Mystery: The Ascension

This is the event we celebrate forty days after Easter on Ascension Thursday. We celebrate Jesus ascending into heaven, body and soul. **(Mark 16:19)**

The Third Glorious Mystery: The Descent of the Holy Spirit

*This is the event when the Holy Spirit came to the apostles and gave them guidance on how they were to live their lives. This was done in the form of tongues of fire. We celebrate this event fifty days after Easter, on Pentecost Sunday. **(Acts of the Apostles 2:4)***

The Fourth Glorious Mystery: The Assumption

*This is the event when Mary, the mother of Jesus, was taken into heaven and was united with her Son Jesus. We celebrate this day every year on August 15. **(Luke 1:48-49)***

The Fifth Glorious Mystery: The Coronation of the Blessed Virgin Mary

*This is the event when Mary was crowned queen of heaven by her Divine Son Jesus. We celebrate this day every year on August 22. **(Revelation 12:1)***

THE JOYFUL MYSTERIES OF THE ROSARY

5

The First Joyful Mystery: The Annunciation

*This is the event when the angel Gabriel announced to Mary that she would be the mother of Jesus. We celebrate this day every year on March 25. **(Luke 1:28-31)***

The Second Joyful Mystery: The Visitation

*This is the event when Mary visited her cousin, Elizabeth, who was pregnant with John the Baptist. We celebrate this day every year on May 31. **(Luke 1:41-42)***

The Third Joyful Mystery: The Nativity

*This is the event of the birth of Jesus. We celebrate this day every year on December 25. **(Luke 2:7)***

The Fourth Joyful Mystery: The Presentation

*This is the event when parents would present their child to God in the temple. We celebrate this day every year on February 2. This is forty days after Christmas. **(Luke 2:22-23)***

The Fifth Joyful Mystery: The Finding of Jesus in the Temple

*This is the event when the parents of Jesus found Him in the temple with teachers, listening to them and asking them questions. We celebrate this day every year on the Sunday between Christmas and New Year's Day. **(Luke 2:46)***

THE LUMINOUS MYSTERIES OF THE ROSARY

5

The First Luminous Mystery: The Baptism of Jesus

*This is the event when Jesus was baptized by John the Baptist in the Jordan River. We celebrate this day every year on January 12. This is nineteen days after His birth. **(Matthew 3:13-17)***

The Second Luminous Mystery: The Wedding of Cana

*This is the event when Jesus changed water into wine. Jesus performed this miracle for the people in need. We celebrate this miracle on the second Sunday after the Epiphany each January. **(John 2:3-5)***

The Third Luminous Mystery: The Proclamation of the Kingdom of God

*This event is when Jesus went to Galilee, proclaiming, "The kingdom of God is at hand. Repent and believe!" We remember this event during Lent when we try to transform our lives and become a holier person. **(Mark 1:15)***

The Fourth Luminous Mystery: The Transfiguration

*This event is when Jesus took Peter, James, and John up a high mountain. There, He was transfigured before them. The appearance of Jesus changed into a beautiful spiritual state. We celebrate this day every year on August 6. **(Matthew 17:2)***

The Fifth Luminous Mystery: The Institution of the Eucharist

*This event is when Jesus offered His body and blood because of His love for humanity. We celebrate this day every year on Holy Thursday. **(John 6:51-56)***

THE SORROWFUL MYSTERIES OF THE ROSARY

5

The First Sorrowful Mystery: The Agony in the Garden

*This is the event when Jesus prayed so hard that His sweat became like blood, and when He came to His disciples, they were asleep. This was at Gethsemane. We remember this sacrifice and suffering during Lent. **(Luke 22:44-45)***

The Second Sorrowful Mystery: The Scourging at the Pillar

*This is the event when Pilate had him scourged, when His body had to suffer from the heavy blows, when He was beaten. We remember this sacrifice and suffering during Lent. **(John 19:1)***

The Third Sorrowful Mystery: The Crowning with Thorns

*This is the event when a crown of thorns was pierced on the head of Jesus. We remember this sacrifice and suffering during Lent. **(Matthew 27:28-29)***

The Fourth Sorrowful Mystery: The Carrying of the Cross

*This is the event when Jesus carried the cross upon His shoulder to Calvary. We remember this sacrifice and suffering during Lent. **(John 19:17)***

The Fifth Sorrowful Mystery: The Crucifixion

*This is the event when Jesus was crucified. He uttered a loud cry and said, "Father, into Your hands, I command my spirit." After he said this, he expired. We remember this sacrifice and suffering during Lent. **(Luke 23:46)***

Praying the rosary as a family can be a very peaceful experience. Reflecting and meditating on all these marvelous events in the life of Jesus and remembering His mother at the same time can be a spiritual memory that lasts forever. I know our children have a wonderful memory of praying the rosary with their grandma and grandpa. They love to share how Grandpa had polka music on in the background that Grandma couldn't hear! My memory of praying the rosary was in our cellar when I was in elementary school. My dad led it. It was when a hail storm was taking place, and at the end, we went out and saw hail in drifts. Hardly anything was said, except for being grateful that no one was hurt. For a lot of years, I was not interested in praying the rosary, and I was even upset because I was told that prayers were answered when you prayed the rosary. For a while, I believed that my prayers were not answered because I had to have a surgery that I never wanted. My prayers were answered because I have received numerous years of feeling very healthy since then. My husband and I pray the rosary often when we travel and every evening when we are at home. We pray it after I have watched Wheel of Fortune *and* America Says. *Our granddaughter recently joined us in praying the rosary. She even led one of the mysteries, and she is only in the second grade. What a joyful experience it was for Grandma and Grandpa!*

What memories do other people have of praying the rosary? What new memories can we make of praying together?

The Cardinal Virtues

4

Fortitude

A story of fortitude is when any parent is sitting in a children's hospital by their helpless loved one, enduring the emotional pain of striving with their child for survival. The courage of their caregivers in the time of such crisis and unknown is the meaning of fortitude.

The volunteers and/or staff who operate the McDonald's homes or Rainbow homes for these families in their time of need are people who join in with empathy and concern for these people.

Justice

A story of justice could include most any court story. The laws are for the good of the people, and those who work in these fields make great effort to strive for justice for the good of all. One example may be those who face charges for driving while intoxicated. This is a danger to the lives of others, and there needs to be consequences for those who do not respect the lives of others. A lot of people think laws like speeding or road sign violations are not that important, but they are there to protect the safety of people.

Prudence

A story of prudence is the ability to govern oneself and discipline oneself by the use of reason. This is when one has careful judgment in whatever circumstance one is in. When a child has tantrums or when an adult is in a bad temper, the provider makes decisions to control the situation in a prudent way.

Temperance

A story of temperance is controlling one's own behavior like when one sees another restraining from alcohol and is inspired by that. Everything in a person is to be directed to the supreme end. One who makes moderate use of things that can be unhealthy for one's body is a person with temperance. Using reason to implement decisions that are good and healthy for the body is temperance.

The Ends (Winds) of the Earth

4

EAST-NORTH-SOUTH-WEST

The Marks of the Church

4

We are one *church. What does that mean?*

Being one church means we all profess the same faith, the same sacrifice, and the same sacraments, and we are united under the same pope.

We are a holy *church. What does that mean?*

Being a holy church means we have a church that was founded by Jesus Christ, who is all holy. It teaches the will of Christ and holy doctrines, and it provides the means of living a holy life.

We are a Catholic *church. What does that mean?*

Being a Catholic church means we are universal because it is destined to last for all time, and it teaches all nations the truths revealed by God.

We are an apostolic *church. What does that mean?*

Being an apostolic church means that the church was founded by Jesus Christ on the apostles and is governed by their lawful successors.
Marks of the church are the clear signs that help all people recognize the true church founded by Christ.

Essential Relationships

3

God - Father
Jesus - Son
Holy Spirit - Guide

God the Father is the One who started all this world and creation! How awesome and beyond our human understanding is that? What kind of relationship does each man or woman have with their God? What kind of vision and dream does each man or woman have for their relationship with God?

Jesus, the Son, is the One who gave His life because of love for us, sinners! How awesome and beyond our understanding is that? What kind of relationship does each man or woman have with Jesus? What kind of vision and dream does each man or woman have for their relationship with Jesus?

The Holy Spirit, the Guide, is the One that protects us and gives us direction on how to live our life! How awesome and beyond our understanding is that? What kind of relationship does each man or woman have with the Holy Spirit? What kind of vision and dream does each man or woman have for their relationship with the Holy Spirit?

Do families spend time in growing in their relationships with the Father, the Son, and the Holy Spirit? A simple formula that could be used when praying spontaneously as a family is

PATS = Praise, Ask, Thanks, and Sorry

The Theological Virtues

Faith Hope Love

There are many events in people's lives that call for faith, hope, and love. A lot of these come at the birth of a child (a miracle). Just to reflect on some of the events of birth, a mother may experience a lot of tiredness and nausea during pregnancy. She has to have several appointments with a doctor. She may even have to be hospitalized because of blood pressure and complications that can come from preeclampsia. The mother may be told to hurry fast when the baby is being born because the baby's cord is around the neck. The mother may be told to hurry because there is no heartbeat in the baby. The mother may be told to wait because the doctor is not there yet. The mother may be told that she will be having an emergency C-section. The mother may be told that her baby will have to have immediate surgery because organs are outside of the baby's body. The mother may be told that her baby is black and blue and does not look well. The mother may be thanking God for every contraction because she is grateful to be able to give birth to a baby and be a part of God's creation. The miracle of life is so precious. How could we ever make fun of God's design of it from the beginning of it to the end of it?

God's creation is such a marvel to contemplate. I remember as a youth riding the horse to bring home the milk cows. I so much enjoyed the horse and then stopping and standing on the horse to eat mulberries off the mulberry trees. Seeing the many different kinds of birds flying through the air was also fascinating, then hard telling what animal might come by and scare the horse, such as a coyote or a rattle snake! This in itself was an experience that took faith, hope, and love; the love of doing the right thing like the chores that needed to be done, the faith in the horse that I would accomplish the task that needed to be done, also the hope that the weather would bring me safely home in time so all that needed to be done would be.

The sickness of a child or the accident of a child sometimes becomes a miracle. When a loved one becomes ill and no one knows how they got well, this is a miracle. When remembering and paying attention to faith and reason, we will be brought to the truth. Faith is built by deeper relationships with God and others. Do we do little things with great love? Goodness and truth work together. Virtues of habit and a firm disposition help us do what is good. Do I talk to Jesus about my hopes? There are numerous reasons to live with faith, hope, and love.

Do we have one hundred reasons for faith?
Do we have one hundred reasons to hope?
Do we have one hundred reasons and one hundred people to love?

Are these written down?

Writing can bring us in contact with our souls. Writing can be a way of saving the graced moments we have with God.

Writing can become a way to begin to express and continue to express your inner thoughts of your relationship with God and others. This can pump up your enthusiasm and energy for your God!

God

1

Qualities of the men in my life: My dad's gratitude was shared often, my brother's generosity is shared often, and my husband's great way of proclaiming the gospel is shared often.

It is my dream and hope that all men and women will reach their final place in peace and joy. Let us work together to step up the ladder one step at a time and not slide to the side or down.

Possible legal laws to promote an ideal man and ideal woman and support family life:

1. Protect the family and the life of respect. Men having being intimate not within the family need at least a ticket equal to a speeding violation. The roads need to be safe to live on, so why not promote homes of families be safe? Men have the gift to begin life and the responsibility of it.
2. Child support should begin at conception. A woman begins her job at conception with feeling sick and having to have doctor's visits, etc.
3. Long-term jail/work time for people who rape and/or harass needs to be enforced with financial payments for the victim. Of course, no consequences would be needed if things were done right in the first place.
4. Abortion clinics need to become homes for the mother and baby of the unwanted pregnancies to be paid for by the father of the child, or we need enough people in this world who would step up and truly become a daddy or mommy in ways that support this unborn baby. Let us be honest about when parents are abandoning their children. Do they realize what they are truly doing? Are we *doing* enough to love these babies/children?

Women who go to abortion clinics are primarily in a state of trauma and do not know and realize what they are doing. They need the right kind of help, but men need to make sure they did not put them in this state of mind and positon in the first place.

Having pleasure rather than being responsible needs to be replaced with the honest real meaning of love by both the woman and the man. From my perspective, those who work in abortion clinics need to be seen as people who may have misunderstandings and misinformation about what they are doing. They may be seeing themselves as a person with empathy trying to stop the pain of another, and/or they may be people committing murders and need to go to jail.

Medical situations in which the physical lives of the woman and her baby are at risk are situations between the doctor and the woman only. These situations are in a different area of respect and study. The experience of working at a birthright helps one be more deeply in touch with the people living in this confused state of mind. Spending time in educating oneself more thoroughly in this area is greatly needed so one can *be* a strong supporter of all life situations and not a judge of people. God is always our judge in every way. What ways do we present ourselves? How can we do the right and good thing as a people and a society?

5. Incentive laws and classes need to be passed to promote abstinence for the good of family life with a balance of the physical and spiritual life. True friendship in relationships needs to be taught and lived, and the respect for life needs to have laws that are in place and enforced at least equal to the laws of stealing. (Beginning a life that is unwanted doesn't even get a ticket equal to a speeding ticket, how sad.)

It would be much better to just get beyond the politics and laws and just *live* the way that is right and good for life in all circumstances and situations!

This book of reflections is for those who read it to hopefully give them an opportunity to bring peace and joy into their families through gaining new or renewed perspectives in their everyday living. It is a book without pictures, so the thoughts of enhancing the story of life for their loved ones won't be distracted. What has been shared has come from others who have made a difference in my life by helping me have purpose and vision in what I do. These people are family, friends, educators, role models, retreat leaders and participants, and even some preachers! How exciting and great life can be here on earth, especially with the hope of that extraordinary life to come! May our hearts be moved as we make our imagination *new* as we reflect on *heaven*! Being present with God will lead us to victory! Because of our humanness, our hearts will be restless until they rest in God. What's the next step? What's the end? What's the goal? It doesn't matter who you are. Even if you are not a spring chicken, there is room to do better!

Meeting the most generous giver of gifts seems pretty awesome! I have been given so much even answers to little and unimportant prayers! My gratitude can never be enough! I hope I can be forgiven when I was not forgiving to those in my life who hurt me and they did not know what they were doing! I need to stop wanting, judging, and whining. I have been so blessed with the love of others in my life, especially those who are so close to being an ideal man or an ideal woman! God is thinking of me! God is allowing me to be! I can experience the greatest gift, God, in my life anytime and anywhere!

In conclusion, please reflect on the question "What is heaven to me?" Let us always be eager to know more and share it and live it! Maybe take an adventure and find more numbers in the Bible! Maybe sneak this book to someone and hope and pray for better lives!

Why 101?

God is our number one in the beginning.
God is our center in the middle.
God is our number one in the end.

101

9 781664 141179